All Color Book of
MAIN COURSES

ARCO PUBLISHING INC.
New York

CONTENTS

Series editor: Mary Lambert

Published 1984 by
Arco Publishing, Inc.
215 Park Avenue South
New York, NY 10003

Library of Congress Catalog
Card Number: 84-70830
ISBN 0-668-06216-9 cloth
ISBN 0-668-06222-3 paper

Printed in Italy

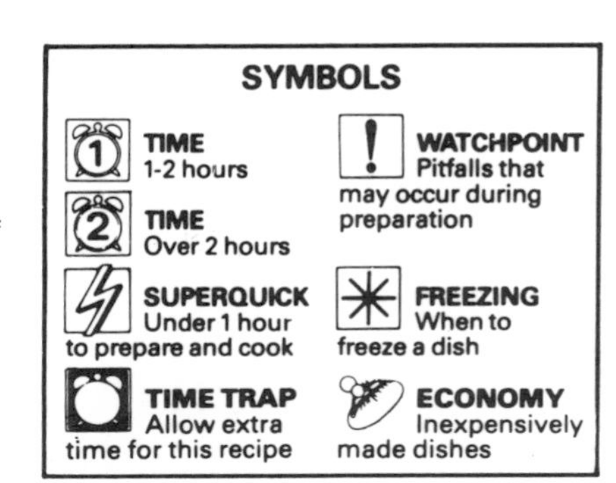

INTRODUCTION

The highlight of any meal is the main course, but it is often hard to achieve the variety of dishes that you would like without spending too much money. This book contains a balanced selection of Pork, Beef and Veal, Lamb, Poultry, Fish and Seafood and Variety Meat dishes to suit all palates – and they don't take ages to make. There are nearly 80 recipes including a mixture of casseroles, dishes with joints of meat and more spicy dishes like *Stir-fried beef with cashews* or *Chicken paprikash*. If you prefer the more traditional dishes you can make *Pot-roasted leg of lamb* or perhaps the tasty *Family fish pie*.

All the recipes contain full color pictures so that you can see from the start how the dish will turn out. They are also calorie-counted and contain cook's notes which give you serving and buying ideas for the dish. They also tell you the timing of the dish and alternative fillings to make it more economic or perhaps spice it up more.

Pork scallops with plums

SERVES 4

8 pork scallops, each weighing 2 oz
1 can (about 1 lb) red plums, drained (see Buying guide)
2 tablespoons vegetable oil
2 tablespoons butter or margarine
1 onion, finely chopped
⅔ cup apple juice or dry white wine
1 teaspoon ground cinnamon
½ teaspoon ground coriander
salt and freshly ground black pepper

1 Carefully remove the pits from the plums, keeping them as whole as possible if using canned ones.

2 Make the sauce: Heat half the oil and half the butter in a pan, add the onion, cook gently 10 minutes until softened. Pour in the juice and bring to a boil. Add the spices and salt and pepper to taste. Stir well, then lower the heat, cover and cook the sauce gently for 5 minutes.

3 Add the plums to the sauce, cover and simmer very gently a further 5 minutes, taking care not to break up the plums. Taste and adjust seasoning.

4 Meanwhile, divide the remaining oil and butter beween 2 large skillets and heat gently. Add the pork scallops and cook over high heat 3 minutes on each side, until browned. [!]

5 To serve, arrange the scallops on a warmed serving dish and spoon over the sauce. Serve at once.

Cook's Notes

TIME
This dish takes 35 minutes to prepare and cook.

WATCHPOINT
Do not overcook or keep the scallops warm as they will toughen. They should be cooked while the sauce and plums are cooking.

BUYING GUIDE
If you use fresh plums you will need ½ lb, pitted and sliced. Add them to the sauce with the juice and cook 10-15 minutes.

● 455 calories per portion

Marinated pork chops

SERVES 4

8 thin pork chops, or 4 thicker chops

MARINADE

4 tablespoons soy sauce
2 tablespoons orange juice
2 tablespoons olive oil or corn oil
2 tablespoons tomato catsup
2 tablespoons light soft brown sugar
1 teaspoon ground ginger
grated rind of 1 orange
salt and freshly ground black pepper
small bunch scallions, thinly sliced

1 Make the marinade: Mix all the ingredients together, including the scallions, making sure the sugar dissolves.

2 Put 4 of the chops in a dish so they do not overlap one another. Spoon over half the marinade, putting a few pieces of scallion on each chop.

3 Put the remaining chops on top and spoon the rest of the marinade over them. Cover with plastic wrap and refrigerate at least 6 hours, basting occasionally.

4 Remove chops from the marinade and broil under high heat about 4 minutes on each side. (Thicker chops will need about 7-8 minutes each side.) Spoon the marinade with the scallions onto the chops when you turn them, so that the scallions become brown and crispy. Serve at once on a warmed serving plate.

Cook's Notes

TIME

Preparation 10 minutes but allow at least 6 hours to marinate the chops. Cooking takes 8-15 minutes.

VARIATIONS

Marinades are infinitely variable. Try substituting lemon juice for the orange juice, or add a splash of wine.

SERVING IDEAS

Serve with new potatoes or boiled potatoes mashed with dairy sour cream and chives plus a simple green salad. Garnish with orange slices.

● 550 calories per portion

Mediterranean pork casserole

SERVES 4

1½-1¾ lb pork loin rib chops, trimmed of bone and fat and cut into small cubes
1 tablespoon vegetable oil
1 onion, sliced
1 clove garlic, crushed (optional)
1-2 teaspoons paprika
¼ teaspoon dried thyme
salt and freshly ground black pepper
1 large green pepper, seeded and cut into strips
1 can (about 14 oz) tomatoes
¼ lb button mushrooms, quartered
2 teaspoons cornstarch

1 Heat the oil in a large flameproof casserole and cook the pork cubes over brisk heat about 5 minutes, stirring continuously. Lower the heat, add the onion and garlic, if using, and cook about 5 minutes until the onion is soft and translucent.

2 Sprinkle over the paprika and thyme and season to taste. Stir in the green pepper, tomatoes and mushrooms and bring to a boil. Lower the heat, cover the pan and simmer gently 1 hour or until the pork is tender, stirring occasionally.

3 Mix the cornstarch to a smooth paste with a little cold water, stir in a spoonful of the hot liquid from the pork, then stir this mixture back into the pork. Bring to a boil, stirring, then simmer 1-2 minutes until thickened. Taste and adjust seasoning. Serve at once, straight from the casserole.

Cook's Notes

TIME
Preparation takes about 30 minutes and cooking just over 1 hour.

COOK'S TIP
This casserole improves in flavor if made a day in advance. It can be kept, covered, in the refrigerator overnight.

BUYING GUIDE
Use lean rib chops for this dish, not the fatter ribs used in Chinese cooking.

VARIATION
If you prefer a slightly spicier flavor, simply add more paprika according to taste.

SERVING IDEAS
Boiled noodles or potatoes plus a bright-colored vegetable such as carrots or broccoli, are good accompaniments to this casserole.

FREEZING
Allow the cooked casserole to cool and then remove the excess fat from the surface. Freeze in a rigid container up to 3 months. Thaw overnight in the refrigerator, then heat through until bubbling.

• 525 calories per portion

Pork ragoût

SERVES 4

- **1¾ lb fresh belly pork, or side of pork trimmed of excess fat, cut into strips 1 inch long and ¾ inch wide**
- **2 tablespoons vegetable oil**
- **1 large onion, chopped**
- **6 tablespoons all-purpose flour**
- **2½ cups chicken broth**
- **4 large carrots, cut into thin slices**
- **thinly pared rind of 1 lemon, cut into strips**
- **¼ lb black-eyed beans, soaked overnight in cold water, drained**
- **½ teaspoon ground coriander**
- **½ teaspoon ground turmeric**
- **¼ teaspoon ground ginger**
- **freshly ground black pepper**
- **salt**
- **strips of lemon rind and chopped parsley to garnish**

1 Preheat the oven to 325°.

2 Heat three-quarters of the oil in a flameproof casserole, add the pork and cook 3-4 minutes until lightly browned and sealed on both sides. Remove with a slotted spoon and drain on paper towels.

3 Heat the remaining oil in the casserole, add the onion and cook gently 5 minutes until soft and lightly colored. Sprinkle in the flour and stir over low heat 1-2 minutes. Gradually stir in broth. Bring to a boil and then simmer, stirring, until thick.

4 Add the carrots, lemon strips, beans and spices, and season to taste with ground black pepper. Bring back to a boil and then boil 10 minutes. Return the meat to the casserole, cover and cook in the oven about 2 hours. 

5 Before serving, add salt and black pepper to taste, and garnish with the strips of lemon rind and the chopped parsley. Serve at once.

Cook's Notes

TIME
30 minutes to prepare and 2 hours to cook.

FREEZING
Cool quickly, then pour into a rigid container. Seal, label and freeze up to 2 months. To serve: Thaw overnight in the refrigerator then reheat in a 350° oven 30 minutes, until the ragoût is bubbling.

DID YOU KNOW
In Classic French cookery, a *ragoût* is a stew made with meat or fish cut into even-sized pieces. These are browned all over first and then simmered in broth.

● 810 calories per portion

Stir-fried pork and cucumber

SERVES 4-6

- 2 lb fresh streaky pork belly slices
- 1 medium cucumber
- 2 tablespoons cornstarch
- 2 tablespoons dry sherry
- 2 tablespoons soy sauce
- 1¼ cups chicken broth
- 2 tablespoons vegetable oil
- 1 clove garlic, finely chopped
- 1 large onion, finely chopped
- 1 teaspoon ground ginger, or ½ teaspoon finely chopped fresh root ginger.

1 Trim the slices of pork of any excess fat. Cut the slices into thin strips about 2 inches long.

2 Wipe but do not pare the cucumber, then cut into quarters lengthwise, trimming off the ends. Scoop out the seeds with a teaspoon. Cut the quarters lengthwise again and cut the pieces into 1-inch lengths.

3 Mix the cornstarch to a paste in a bowl, with a little of the sherry or soy sauce, then stir in the remainder with the broth.

4 Put the oil and garlic into a skillet and set over high heat until the garlic sizzles.

5 Add the pork and cook over high heat about 15 minutes until all the pieces are crisp and well browned, stirring briskly all the time.

6 Pour all but about 1 tablespoon of the fat from skillet and then set the pan back over low heat.

7 Stir in the cucumber, onion and ginger and cook, stirring, about 5 minutes until the onion is translucent.

8 Give the cornstarch mixture a stir and pour it into the pan. Increase the heat and bring the mixture to a boil. Cook over high heat 3 minutes until a thick, translucent sauce is formed.

9 Transfer to a warmed serving dish and serve at once.

Cook's Notes

TIME

40 minutes to prepare and cook.

SERVING IDEAS

Serve with a mixture of boiled Chinese noodles and lightly fried beansprouts topped with finely chopped scallions.

BUYING GUIDE

Streaky pork slices are cut from the belly of the pig and are often simply described as "belly pork". You can buy streaky pork in the piece as a cut for roasting, but for this dish the meat needs to be cut into slices. Most butchers sell ready-prepared slices, but if not, ask your butcher to cut them for you and bone them at the same time. Remember too, that the thick end of belly pork (from the middle of the pig) has far more meat on it than the thin end, so it is worth asking for.

● 935 calories per portion

Baked honey ribs

SERVES 4

3 lb pork spare ribs, Chinese style (see Buying guide)
4 tablespoons clear honey
3 tablespoons light brown sugar
1 tablespoon Worcestershire sauce
2 tablespoons tomato catsup
1 tablespoon Dijon-style mustard
2 tablespoons red wine vinegar
salt and freshly ground black pepper

1 Preheat the oven to 400°.

2 If necessary, cut through the ribs to separate them. Put them in a single layer in 1 large or 2 small roasting pans.

3 Combine the remaining ingredients in a small saucepan and season well with salt and pepper. Heat gently over low heat until just simmering.

4 Brush the ribs with the sauce on both sides, using a pastry or similar kitchen brush, then pour over any remaining syrup, making sure the ribs are well coated.

5 Bake in the oven uncovered, 1 hour, basting and turning the ribs frequently then turn the oven down to low, and bake 30 minutes more, or until the flesh is well cooked and the ribs thoroughly coated in syrupy sauce. Serve at once.

Cook's Notes

TIME
Preparation 15 minutes.
Cooking 1½ hours.

BUYING GUIDE
Most butchers will supply sheets of Chinese-style spare ribs, but some need a few days notice. Ordinary spare rib chops will not make a satisfactory substitute.

• 310 calories per portion

COOK'S TIP
Marinate the ribs in the sauce ingredients for a few hours, before barbecuing them, basting with the sauce.

SERVING IDEAS
Eat the ribs with your fingers (making sure you have plenty of napkins on hand). Excellent accompaniments for these honey ribs are hot Greek pita bread and fresh green salad.

Pork fillet in puff pastry

SERVES 4-6

2 pieces pork fillet (tenderloin), each weighing about ¾ lb
1 tablespoon vegetable oil
1 sheet (½ of 17 oz package) frozen puff pastry, thawed
⅓ cup button mushrooms, sliced
1 dessert apple

STUFFING

½ cup fresh white bread crumbs
1 tablespoon vegetable shortening
1 small onion, grated
1 teaspoon dried sage
salt and freshly ground black pepper
1 egg, beaten

1 Preheat the oven to 400°.

2 Slit the pork fillets ready for stuffing (see Preparation).

3 Heat the oil in a large skillet and cook the fillets over moderate heat until they are lightly browned. Remove from the skillet and drain on paper towels.

4 To make the stuffing: Put the bread crumbs in a bowl with the shortening, onion and sage, and season with salt and pepper. Add enough egg to bind the mixture, reserving the remaining egg for sealing and glazing the pastry.

5 Roll out the pastry thinly on a floured surface to make a rectangle measuring about 16 × 12 inches. Trim edges of the pastry and reserve for decorating. Place the pastry on a dampened cookie sheet.

6 Place 1 pork fillet in the center of the pastry and sprinkle the mushrooms over it. Pare, core and grate the apple and sprinkle over the mushrooms Place the second pork fillet on top of mushroom and apple layer and spread the stuffing mixture over this.

7 Fold over the ends of the pastry then the sides, so that the meat is enclosed in a pastry parcel with the join on the top. Seal the edges with some of the reserved egg.

8 Decorate along the seam of the parcel with pastry leaves made from the trimmings. Brush with the remaining beaten egg and bake in the oven 40 minutes until the pastry has risen and is golden. Transfer to a warmed serving dish and serve at once.

Cook's Notes

TIME
Total preparation and cooking time is 50 minutes.

SERVING IDEAS
Serve with broccoli, or Brussels sprouts sprinkled with ground mace and mushroom sauce.

PREPARATION
To cut the pork fillet so that it is ready for the stuffing:

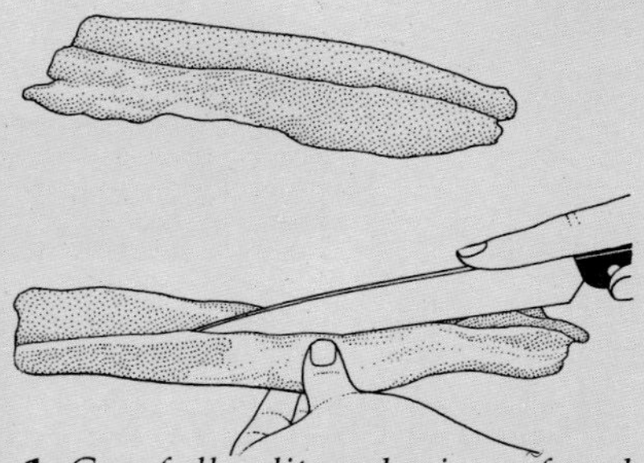

1 *Carefully slit each piece of pork fillet (tenderloin) without cutting right through. Open out each piece flat so that there are 2 rectangular pieces of meat, each about 20 cm/8 inches long and 13 cm/5 inches wide.*

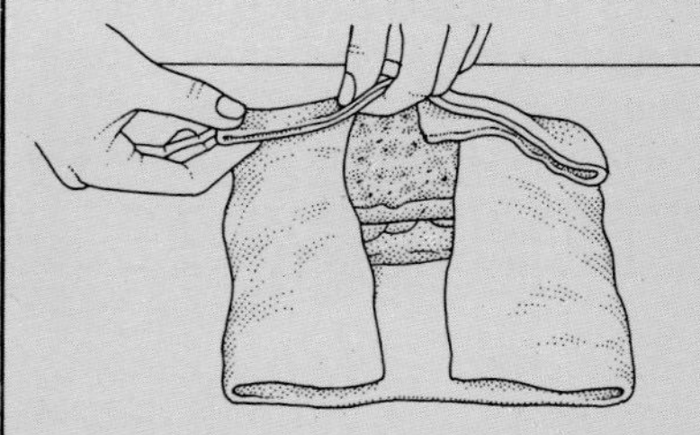

2 *Make a pastry parcel around the meat and stuffing to enclose it completely.*

●805 calories/3375 kj per portion

Roast pork with peaches

SERVES 4

2½ lb boned pork roast (see Buying guide)
salt
1 tablespoon vegetable oil

STUFFED PEACHES

4 ripe fresh peaches, peeled (see Preparation)
2 tablespoons lemon juice
2 tablespoons butter or margarine
⅓ cup fresh white bread crumbs
1 onion, finely chopped
2 celery stalks, finely chopped
1 teaspoon dried sage
½ teaspoon grated lemon rind
freshly ground black pepper
1 teaspoon grated Parmesan cheese

1 Preheat the oven to 375°.
2 Using a sharp knife, score the skin of the pork at ¼-inch intervals, cutting into the fat below the skin but not into the meat.
3 Wipe the pork dry with paper towels. Sprinkle skin liberally with salt and rub it in with the oil.
4 Place the pork in a small roasting pan and roast in the oven 1 hour.
5 Meanwhile, prepare the stuffed peaches. Halve the peaches, remove the pits and sprinkle the cut sides of fruit with a little lemon juice.
6 Melt the butter in a small saucepan, add the bread crumbs, onion and celery and cook gently 4-5 minutes, stirring constantly to prevent sticking. Remove from the heat and add the sage, lemon rind and 1 tablespoon lemon juice. Mix the ingredients together and season well with salt and pepper.
7 Place 1 tablespoonful of the stuffing in the hollow of each peach and smooth over with a knife. Sprinkle lightly with the Parmesan cheese.
8 When the pork has cooked 1 hour, remove the roasting pan from the oven, and place the stuffed peaches around the pork. Return to the oven a further 30 minutes or until the pork is tender, basting once with the drippings in the pan. Transfer the pork to a warmed serving platter and surround with the stuffed peaches. Serve at once.

Cook's Notes

TIME
Preparation of pork, 5 minutes, then 30 minutes to prepare the stuffed peaches once the pork is in the oven. Cooking 1½ hours.

BUYING GUIDE
Cuts suitable for this recipe are: Any boned rolled roast from the loin, leg, shoulder, belly or spareribs. Ask your butcher to bone the joint for you and to tie it into a neat shape.

PREPARATION
To peel the peaches, immerse in very hot water for 1 minutes. Drain then nick the skin near the stem and peel away the skin.

● 740 calories per portion

Hawaiian pork parcels

SERVES 4

4 thick pork loin rib chops weighing about ⅓-½ lb.
1 can (about 1 lb) pineapple rings in natural juice, drained with juice reserved (see Economy)
1 tablespoon butter or margarine
1 small onion, chopped
1 cup fresh whole wheat bread crumbs
1 teaspoon cider vinegar
1 tablespoon finely chopped fresh parsley
dash of hot-pepper sauce
salt and freshly ground black pepper
parsley sprigs, to garnish

SAUCE

1 tablespoon cornstarch
⅔ cup chicken broth
1 teaspoon Worcestershire sauce
1 teaspoon cider vinegar

1 Cut 4 squares of foil each large enough to contain a chop easily.

2 Using a sharp knife, slit each pork chop horizontally, from the fatty outside edge to the bone, without cutting all the way through, to make a small pocket.

3 Make the stuffing (see Cook's tips): Chop 1 pineapple ring finely. Melt the butter in a skillet, add the onion and cook gently 5 minutes until soft and lightly colored. In a bowl combine the onion mixture with the chopped pineapple, bread crumbs, vinegar, 1 tablespoon pineapple juice, the parsley and pepper sauce. Season thoroughly with salt and pepper.

4 Preheat the broiler to moderate. Preheat the oven to 375°.

5 Divide the stuffing mixture into 4 portions. Using a teaspoon, spoon a portion of stuffing into the pocket of each chop. Broil the chops about 5 minutes on each side, until lightly browned (see Cook's tips).

6 Place a chop on each piece of foil and top each with a pineapple ring. Fold over the edges of the foil to make a loose parcel, then seal the edges tightly.

7 Arrange the parcels in a large, shallow roasting pan and bake in the oven about 50 minutes, or until the juices run clear when the meat is pierced with a fine skewer.

8 About 5 minutes before the end of cooking time, make the sauce: Measure out ⅔ cups of the reserved pineapple juice into a saucepan. In a cup, blend the cornstarch with a little of the measured pineapple juice stirring all the time to make a smooth paste. Stir the mixture into the pineapple juice with the broth, Worcestershire sauce and vinegar, and season to taste with salt and pepper. Bring slowly to a boil, stirring, until the sauce is thickened and smooth.

9 Remove the Hawaiian pork chops from their foil parcels and place them on a warmed serving plate. Garnish each pork chop with a sprig of parsley placed in the center of the pineapple ring. Pass the sauce in a warmed gravyboat.

Cook's Notes

TIME
Preparation 25 minutes, cooking 1 hour.

COOK'S TIPS
The stuffing may be made a day ahead and kept in the refrigerator.

Turn the chops carefully with a turner, so that none of the stuffing comes out.

ECONOMY
Use the remaining pineapple rings in a fruit salad or with ice cream.

● 445 calories per portion

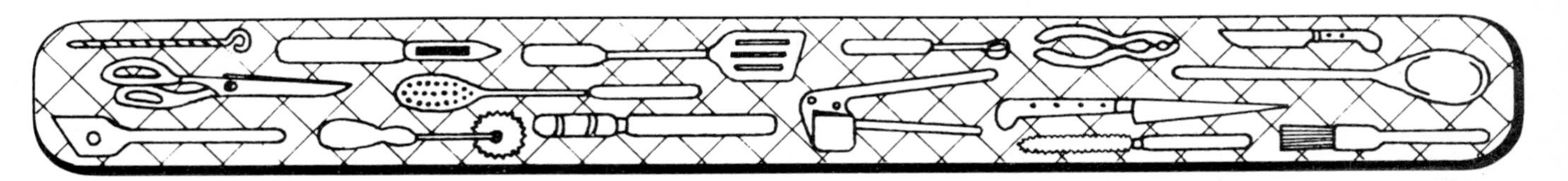

Pork and pears

SERVES 4

4 pork loin rib chops, trimmed of fat and rind
2 tablespoons butter or margarine
salt and freshly ground black pepper
1 can (about 15 oz) pear halves
1 tablespoon chopped fresh marjoram, or 1½ teaspoons dried marjoram
1 tablespoon lemon juice

1 Preheat the oven to 375°.
2 Melt the butter in a large skillet. Add the chops and cook for 3-4 minutes on each side until golden brown.
3 Remove with a slotted spoon and place in a single layer in an ovenproof dish. Sprinkle with salt and pepper to taste. Drain the pears, reserving the juice, and cook in the hot fat about 10 minutes until brown. Place on top of the chops in the dish.
4 Pour the reserved pear juice into the pan and stir with a wooden spoon to dislodge any sediment at the bottom. Add the marjoram and lemon juice, and raise the heat. Bring to a boil and boil rapidly, stirring frequently, for about 5 minutes until reduced by about half. [!] Pour over the chops and pears, then cover the dish.
5 Bake in the oven for 25 minutes or until the chops are tender. Transfer to a warmed serving dish and serve at once.

Cook's Notes

TIME
25 minutes preparation, 25 minutes to cook.

VARIATION
Try canned apricot halves, or pineapple rings instead of pears.

WATCHPOINT
When reducing the pear juice, do not boil for longer than 5 minutes or it will become too thick and syrupy at this stage and not coat the chops and pears. It will reduce further during baking in the oven.

SERVING
Good accompaniments are cauliflower or leeks, lightly boiled then drained and tossed with butter and about ¼ cup chopped flaked almonds.

● 490 calories per portion

Quick Portuguese pork

SERVES 4

1½ lb pork fillets (tenderloin), sliced into thin strips
1 large grapefruit (see Cook's tip)
2 teaspoons ground coriander
salt and freshly ground black pepper
3 tablespoons olive oil
4 tablespoons dry white wine
1 can (about 6 oz) pimientos, drained and cut into strips (see Buying guide)

1 Grate the rind from the grapefruit and reserve. Remove all the remaining rind and pith, then divide the flesh into segments, cutting away all membranes.

2 Put the strips of pork in a bowl, sprinkle with the ground coriander, the reserved grated rind of the grapefruit and salt and pepper to taste and turn the meat over until thoroughly coated.

3 Heat the oil in a skillet until very hot. Add the pork and cook briskly turning from time to time until evenly browned on all sides. Lower the heat.

4 Pour the juice from a quarter of the grapefruit segments through a strainer. Add to the skillet and stir in the wine and pimientos. Cook 3-4 minutes until the pork is tender, stirring all the time.

5 Transfer the pork and pimientos to a warmed serving dish with a slotted spoon. Keep hot in the lowest possible oven.

6 Bring the liquid in the pan to a boil and boil rapidly until reduced slightly. Lower the heat, add the remaining grapefruit segments and heat through.

7 Remove the grapefruit segments from the pan with a slotted spoon and reserve. Pour the pan juices over the pork and pimientos, then garnish with the reserved grapefruit segments. Serve at once.

Cook's Notes

TIME
10 minutes preparation, 15 minutes to cook.

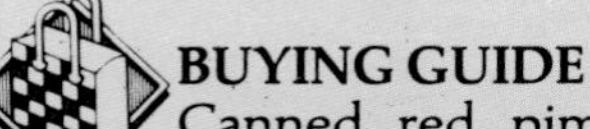

BUYING GUIDE
Canned red pimientos are available from most supermarkets. They are small, sweet peppers, and the fact that they are ready-skinned and sliced makes them a handy pantry shelf item. If you prefer to use a fresh red pepper for this dish, cut it into strips, discarding the white membrane and seeds. Plunge into boiling water 2–3 minutes then refresh under cold running water.

COOK'S TIP
All citrus friuts are easier to grate if they have been thoroughly chilled.

● 400 calories per portion

Dynasty pork

SERVES 4

1½ lb lean stewing pork, trimmed and cut into 1-inch cubes
4 tablespoons all-purpose flour
salt and freshly ground black pepper
2 tablespoons vegetable oil
2 tablespoons butter or margarine
1 onion, chopped
1 green pepper, seeded and sliced
1 clove garlic, crushed (optional)
1¼ cups chicken broth
1 can (about 11 oz) mandarin orange segments, drained, with syrup reserved
1 tablespoon wine vinegar
1 tablespoon soy sauce
2 tomatoes, peeled and chopped

1 Put the flour in a plastic bag and season with salt and pepper. Place the pork in the bag and shake until the meat is well coated with flour. Reserve any flour remaining in the bag.

2 Heat the oil and butter in a flameproof casserole, add the onion, green pepper and garlic, if using, and cook over gentle heat 5 minutes until the onion is soft and lightly colored. Remove with a slotted spoon and set aside.

3 Add the pork to the pan together with any flour remaining in the bag. Cook over brisk heat 4–5 minutes, turning constantly until browned on all sides.

4 Gradually blend in the chicken broth, mandarin orange syrup, vinegar and soy sauce. Return the cooked vegetables to the pan, bring to a boil and simmer 2-3 minutes, stirring constantly. Add salt and pepper to taste.

5 Lower the heat,cover the pan and simmer very gently for about 1½ hours or until the pork is tender. Add the orange segments and chopped tomatoes and cook a further 5 minutes. Taste and adjust seasoning, then transfer to a warmed serving dish. Serve hot.

Cook's Notes

TIME
Preparation 25 minutes, cooking 1½-1¾ hours.

FREEZING
Transfer the cooked dish to a foil container, cool quickly, then remove any excess solidified fat. Seal, label and freeze up to 6 months. To serve: Reheat from frozen in a 375° oven 1 hour or until bubbling.

PRESSURE COOKING
Do not add flour until end of cooking time. Bring to high (H) pressure and cook 15 minutes. Release pressure quickly. Blend flour with a little fruit syrup, and stir in with tomatoes and orange segments. Bring to a boil and simmer 2 minutes.

• 710 calories per portion

Fruity stuffed pork chops

SERVES 4

4 thick pork loin chops (see Buying guide)
2 tablespoons vegetable oil

STUFFING

1 tablespoon butter or margarine
1 small onion chopped
⅓ cup prunes, soaked overnight, pits removed and finely chopped
1 small dessert apple, pared, cored and grated
½ cup walnuts, roughly chopped
½ cup soft day-old white bread crumbs
salt and freshly ground black pepper
1 small egg, beaten

1 Preheat the oven to 375°.
2 Make the stuffing: Melt the butter in a skillet, add the onion and cook gently 5 minutes until soft and lightly colored. Put the prunes in a bowl with the apple, walnuts and bread crumbs and stir in the onion. Season with salt and pepper and stir in the egg to bind.
3 Using a sharp knife, slit each pork chop horizontally, from the fatty outside edge to the bone, without cutting all the way through. Fill the chops with the stuffing mixture and secure the slit edges with wooden toothpicks.
4 Brush a baking or roasting pan with half the oil. Put in the chops and brush with the remaining oil.
5 Cook the chops in the oven about 20 minutes, then cover the dish with foil and return to the oven 30-40 minutes longer until cooked through. Remove toothpicks to serve.

TIME
Preparing the stuffing and the chops takes about 25 minutes. Allow overnight soaking for the prunes. Cooking in the oven takes 50-60 minutes.

BUYING GUIDE
Choose as thick chops as possible and with as little bone as possible.

COOK'S TIP
If there is any stuffing left over, put it in a small ovenproof dish, cover with foil and bake in the oven below the chops 20 minutes.

● 465 calories per portion

Pork and peas

SERVES 4

2 lb boneless shoulder of pork, trimmed and cut into ½-inch cubes
1¾ cups shelled fresh peas
salt
1 tablespoon vegetable shortening
1 large onion, finely chopped
1 clove garlic, finely chopped (optional)
2 teaspoons paprika
¼ teaspoons cayenne
½ cup hot chicken broth
⅓ cup dry white wine
2 tablespoons chopped fresh parsley

1 Cook the peas in boiling salted water 10 minutes.

2 Meanwhile, melt the shortening in a large skillet, add the pork and cook over brisk heat 5 minutes until browned on all sides. Remove from the pan with a slotted spoon and set aside.

3 Lower the heat and stir in the onion, garlic, if using, paprika and cayenne. Raise the heat to moderate and cook 5 minutes until the onion is soft.

4 Drain the peas, then add to pan with the pork. Stir well, pour in broth and wine. Bring to a boil.

5 Lower the heat, then cover the pan and simmer 40 minutes or until the pork is tender. ✳

6 Taste and adjust seasoning and the parsley then transfer the pork and peas to a warmed serving dish and serve at once, while piping hot.

Cook's Notes

TIME
Total preparation and cooking time 1¼ hours.

FREEZING
Transfer the pork and peas to a rigid container, cool quickly, then seal, label and freeze up to 2 months. To serve: Reheat from frozen until heated through and bubbling. Stir frequently and add a little broth or water if the mixture sticks.

COOK'S TIP
To use frozen peas, do not thaw, simply stir into pan in last 10 minutes.

PRESSURE COOKING
Heat the shortening in the base of cooker, cook the onion, then remove and drain. Cook pork and, if very fatty, drain off excess fat. Return onion and pork to pressure cooker, add liquid (½ cup chicken broth and ⅓ cup white wine) and bring to a boil. Skim liquid if necessary, then bring to high (H) pressure and cook 12 minutes. Reduce pressure quickly, add peas. Bring back to high (H) pressure and cook a further 3 minutes. Reduce pressure quickly.

• 700 calories per portion

Stilton steak

SERVES 4

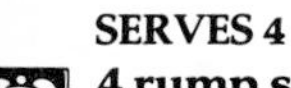

4 rump steaks, each weighing ½ lb (see Buying guide)
1 tablespoon finely chopped onion
1 tablespoon Worcestershire sauce
⅓ cup vegetable oil
¼ cup port or sweet sherry
freshly ground black pepper
1 bay leaf, crumbled
⅔ cup grated Blue Stilton cheese
watercress sprigs and tomato slices, to garnish

1 Put the steaks in a large shallow dish. Combine the onion, Worcestershire sauce, oil, port, pepper and bay leaf and pour over the steaks. Cover and leave to marinate at least 3 hours at room temperature, turning the steaks several times.
2 Line broiler pan with foil, and preheat the broiler to moderate.
3 Using a turner lift the steaks from the marinade and arrange them on the broiler rack. Broil 5-8 minutes, depending on whether you like your steak medium or well done, basting from time to time with the marinade. Turn the steaks and broil another 2-5 minutes.
4 Sprinkle the Stilton over each steak, dividing it equally between them and pressing down with the back of the spoon. Broil a further 3 minutes until the Stilton topping is melted and bubbling.
5 Transfer the steaks to a warmed serving dish, garnish with watercress and tomato and serve at once.

Cook's Notes

TIME
Allow at least 3 hours marinating time. Cooking takes about 15 minutes.

BUYING GUIDE
Rump steak is cut from the lower part of the sirloin. Choose rump steaks that have a slightly purplish tinge which shows that they have been well aged and will be tender. Some supermarkets sell smallish pieces of rump steak in special economy packs: These would be ideal.
Chuck steaks which are much cheaper than rump steak, may be used instead; they will need to be cooked for slightly longer.

COOK'S TIP
If steaks are marinated there is no need to beat the meat to tenderize it. The alcohol in the marinade will break down fibers of the meat.

SERVING IDEAS
Serve the steaks with baked or new potatoes and a green salad.

● 380 calories per portion

Steak and parsnip pie

SERVES 4
1½ lb chuck steak, cut into bite-sized pieces
2 tablespoons vegetable oil
1 large onion, sliced
4 tablespoons all-purpose flour
1 can (about 14 oz) tomatoes
1 chicken bouillon cube
bouquet garni
salt and freshly ground black pepper
½lb parsnips, cut into chunky pieces
1 sheet (½ of 17 oz package) frozen puff pastry, thawed
a little beaten egg, to glaze

Cook's Notes

TIME

Preparation time is 15 minutes. Cooking time is 2¾ hours but remember to allow time for the pastry to thaw.

• 675 calories per portion

VARIATIONS

You could use shoulder or stewing steak, in which case the meat will need longer to cook. Turnips, carrots or rutabagas can be used instead of the parsnips or try using a mixture of root vegetables.

1 Preheat the oven to 350°.

2 Heat the oil in a flameproof casserole, add the meat and onion and cook until the onion is soft and the meat is browned on all sides. Sprinkle in the flour, then cook 1-2 minutes, stirring constantly.

3 Stir in the tomatoes and their juice, crumble in the bouillon cube and stir well to mix. Add the bouquet garni and season to taste with salt and pepper. Bring to a boil, stirring, then cover and transfer to the oven. Cook 1½ hours or until the meat is just tender.

4 Stir in the parsnips and cook a further 45 minutes.

5 Meanwhile, roll out the pastry on a floured surface to a shape slightly larger than the circumference of a deep pie dish or baking dish. Cut off a long narrow strip of pastry all around the edge. Reserve this and other trimmings.

6 Transfer the meat and parsnip mixture to the pie dish, then discard the bouquet garni and taste and adjust seasoning. Increase the oven temperature to 425°. Brush the rim of the pie dish with water, then press the narrow strip of pastry all around the rim. Brush the strip with a little more water, then place the large piece of pastry on top. Trim the edge of the pastry, then knock up and flute.

7 Make leaves or other shapes with the pastry trimmings, then place on top of the pie, brushing the underneath with water so that they do not come off during baking. Make a small hole in the center of the pie for the steam to escape, then brush all over the pastry with beaten egg.

8 Bake the pie in the oven 25–30 minutes until the pastry is well risen and golden brown. Serve hot.

Marinated summer beef

SERVES 4

1½-2 lb roasting beef (see Buying guide)
⅓ cup vegetable oil
⅔ cup dry white wine
1 teaspoon mild Dijon-style mustard
1 teaspoon dried thyme
1 tablespoon lemon juice
1 clove garlic, crushed (optional)
salt and freshly ground black pepper
1 small onion, finely sliced

SALAD
2 potatoes
¼ lb green beans, fresh or frozen
2 carrots, grated
2 tomatoes, quartered

GARNISH
8-10 black olives
1 tablespoon chopped fresh parsley

1 Preheat the oven to 350°.
2 Wrap the beef in foil and place in a roasting pan. Roast in the oven about 1 hour (see Cook's tips). Remove from the oven and leave the beef, still wrapped in foil, to cool about 45 minutes.
3 Make the marinade: Put the oil, wine, mustard, thyme, lemon juice and garlic, if using, in a bowl or in a blender. Season with salt and pepper and beat well with a fork, or process in the blender for 30 seconds.
4 Slice the cooled beef into even, neat slices and arrange them in a shallow dish. Arrange the onion slices on top of the beef and pour over the marinade. Cover the dish of beef with plastic wrap and refrigerate at least 5-6 hours or overnight if possible.
5 Make the salad: Cook the potatoes in boiling salted water 15—20 minutes or until just tender. Drain, cool slightly and cut into bite-sized chunks. Meanwhile, cook the beans in boiling salted water 5-10 minutes or until just tender. Drain well and mix with the potatoes in a bowl. While the vegetables are still warm, pour over 2 tablespoons of the marinade from the beef and gently, turn them with a fork, without breaking them up, to coat thoroughly with the marinade. Cover and chill in the refrigerator 1 hour.
6 When ready to serve, mix the grated carrots and the tomatoes with the potatoes and beans. Remove the meat slices from the marinade, draining off any excess marinade from the slices. Remove the onions from the marinade with a slotted spoon and mix them into the mixed vegetables.
7 Pile the vegetable salad into the center of a serving platter and arrange the marinated beef slices around it. Garnish the platter with black olives and chopped parsley. Serve at once.

Cook's Notes

TIME
Cooking the beef takes about 1 hour. Allow 5-6 hours or overnight for marinating the beef. Preparing the vegetable salad, including cooking the potatoes and beans, takes about 30 minutes. Allow 1 hour for chilling the salad.

BUYING GUIDE
Most supermarkets have a selection of roasting beef cuts. Choose one that is lean and without gristle. Beef ribeye would be a good choice for this dish, or top round roast, which is slightly less expensive.

COOK'S TIPS
How long you cook the beef depends on whether you like it rare or well done, but this dish is most attractive if the meat is still pink. A cut of this weight will be just turning from pink after 1 hour's cooking. Cook only 50 minutes if you like you beef rare, and for 1¼ hours if you like a roast to be well done.

• 440 calories per portion

Tasty hamburgers

SERVES 4
1½ lb lean ground beef
1 small onion, finely grated
1 tablespoon tomato catsup
salt and freshly ground black pepper
⅔ cup mashed Danish Blue cheese
2 tablespoons vegetable oil

1 In a large bowl, mix together the ground beef, onion and tomato catsup and season well with salt and pepper. ✳ Cover the mixture and refrigerate 1 hour.
2 Divide the mashed cheese into 4 portions. Shape each portion into a ball and flatten slightly. Divide the chilled beef mixture into 4 portions and mold 1 portion around each ball of cheese. Shape into a fairly thick hamburger, making sure that the cheese is completely enclosed by the meat mixture.
3 Heat the oil in a large skillet, add the hamburgers and cook about 5-8 minutes on each side, until they are done to your liking.
4 Remove the hamburgers from the pan with a turner, drain quickly on paper towels and serve at once (see Serving ideas).

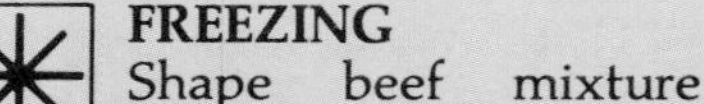

TIME
Preparation takes 10 minutes but allow 1 hour chilling time. Cooking then takes 10-15 minutes.

FREEZING
Shape beef mixture around the cheese as in stage 2. Open freeze hamburgers until solid, then wrap individually in foil and pack together in a freezer bag. Seal, label and return to the freezer up to 3 months. To serve: Thaw at room temperature, then proceed from the beginning of stage 3.

VARIATIONS
Grated sharp Cheddar cheese or finely shredded mozzarella may be substituted for the Danish Blue.
Add a few drops of hot-pepper sauce to the ground beef mixture, for a more piquant taste.

SERVING IDEAS
Serve in the traditional sesame bun with lettuce, sliced tomato and various relishes or mustard. Alternatively, serve with French fried potatoes, without the bun.

● 415 calories per portion

Pot roast brisket

SERVES 4
2 lb fresh brisket of beef, rolled and tied (see Buying guide)
2 tablespoons butter or margarine
1 onion, quartered
2 large carrots, sliced
2 celery stalks, sliced
2 cups beef broth
½ teaspoon dried thyme
½ teaspoon dried marjoram
1 tablespoon soy sauce
freshly ground black pepper
4 teaspoons cornstarch
salt

1 Melt the butter in a large flameproof casserole and cook the brisket over high heat until browned on all sides. Transfer to a plate.
2 Add the onion, carrots and celery to the pan, lower the heat and cook gently 5 minutes, stirring. Return the meat to the pan and add the broth, thyme, marjoram, soy sauce and freshly ground black pepper to taste.
3 Bring to a boil, then lower the heat, cover and simmer gently 2½ hours, turning the meat over every 30 minutes. [!]
4 When tender, remove the meat from the pan and keep warm.
5 Blend the cornstarch to a paste with a little cold water, stir into the pan and bring to a boil. Lower the heat and simmer 2-3 minutes, stirring constantly, then mash the onions, carrots and celery into the gravy in the pan with a potato masher. Taste and adjust seasoning.
6 Place the meat on a warmed serving platter, cutting a few thin slices from one end, if wished. Pour over a little of the gravy, then serve at once, with the remaining gravy passed separately in a gravy boat.

Cook's Notes

TIME
20 minutes preparation; 2½ hours cooking turning the meat every 30 minutes. Allow an extra 5-10 minutes to finish the gravy and slice the meat.

BUYING GUIDE
Make sure you buy a fresh brisket, not a salted one. Look for a good, lean piece.

PRESSURE COOKING
Calculate the cooking time at 12 minutes per 1 lb meat. Remove the trivet from the pressure cooker pan. Brown the meat and vegetables in the pan as described, then add the broth and flavorings. Cover with the lid, bring up to pressure according to manufacturer's instructions, then cook at high (H) pressure for the calculated cooking time (about 50 minutes). Reduce pressure with cold water, lift out the meat and thicken the gravy as described.

WATCHPOINT
To turn the brisket over without splashing or burning yourself, use 2 large kitchen forks, or a fork and a wooden spoon. Make sure you have a firm grip on the meat before you lift it; if it slips back into the pan the hot broth will splash dangerously.

● 505 calories per portion

Flemish beef casserole

SERVES 4

1½ lb chuck steak, trimmed and cut into 1-inch cubes
3 tablespoons vegetable oil
3 medium onions, sliced
¼ lb smoked streaky bacon, chopped
1 clove garlic, crushed (optional)
2 tablespoons all-purpose flour
½ pint beer or ale
⅓ cup beef broth
1 tablespoon red wine vinegar
1 tablespoon light brown sugar
bouquet garni (parsley, thyme, bay leaf)
salt and freshly ground black pepper
1 tablespoon finely chopped parsley, to garnish

MUSTARD CROUTONS

2 large slices white bread, crusts removed, each cut into 4 triangles or squares
2 teaspoons prepared English mustard
vegetable oil, for frying

1 In a large saucepan or flameproof casserole, heat the oil over fairly high heat, and cook the meat, a few pieces at a time, until evenly brown all over. Remove with a slotted spoon to a plate and keep warm.

2 Reduce the heat and cook the onions and bacon, stirring occasionally, 5-7 minutes until softened and beginning to color. Add the garlic, if using, and cook 1 minute.

3 Add the flour and stir, scraping the crusty bits off the bottom of the pan. Cook until it begins to brown. Stir in the beer and broth and bring to a boil, stirring. Return the meat to the pan, then add the remaining ingredients, except the parsley. Stir well, reduce the heat, cover and simmer gently over low heat 1¾-2 hours until the meat is tender.

4 Spread both sides of the bread triangles or squares with mustard.

5 Heat oil in a skillet and cook the croutons for a few seconds until evenly browned on all sides.

6 Drain on paper towels.

7 When the meat is tender, check and adjust seasoning. ✳ Serve hot, garnished with parsley and the mustard croutons.

Cook's Notes

TIME
Preparation 25 minutes, cooking 2 hours.

BUYING GUIDE
Ready-made bouquet garnis are available from most good supermarkets and delicatessens. Remember to remove before serving.

FREEZING
Cool quickly, remove any excess solidified fat and pack in a rigid container or heavy-duty freezer bag. Seal, label and freeze up to 3 months. To use, thaw gently over low heat, bring to boiling point and cook about 20 minutes until thoroughly heated.

COOK'S TIPS
This casserole can be cooked in the oven at 350° for the same length of time.

Like most casseroles, the flavor is improved if it is made one day, cooled, then reheated thoroughly the next day.

ECONOMY
If you use a cheaper cut of stewing steak, such as shin beef, the dish will be less expensive, but remember to trim away all the fat and gristle. Shin beef is tougher than chuck and will need to cook at least an hour longer.

● 620 calories per portion

Mexican beef

SERVES 4

1 lb ground beef (see Buying guide)
1-2 tablespoons vegetable oil
1 small onion, finely chopped
3-4 teaspoons chili seasoning
2 tablespoons quick-cooking oatmeal
1¼ cups beef broth
1 tablespoon tomato paste
pinch of freshly ground nutmeg
salt and freshly ground black pepper
1 can (about 12 oz) whole kernel corn with sweet peppers, drained
1 large or 2 medium avocados
1 tablespoon lemon juice
¼ lb Cheddar cheese, cut into 1-inch cubes

1 Heat 1 tablespoon oil in a heavy-based saucepan. Add the beef and cook over moderate heat 3 minutes, stirring constantly until all the beef has browned, breaking up any lumps with a wooden spoon. Remove the beef with a slotted spoon. Add the onion to the pan and cook 5 minutes until soft and lightly colored, adding a further tablespoon oil if necessary, to prevent overbrowning.

2 Return the beef to the pan, stir in 3 teaspoons chili seasoning, then the oatmeal, broth, tomato paste, nutmeg, salt to taste and add a light sprinkling of pepper.

3 Bring to a boil, stirring, then reduce the heat, cover and simmer gently 40–45 minutes or until the oatmeal is soft and the meat cooked.

4 Stir the drained corn and peppers into the beef mixture and continue to cook, uncovered, 5 minutes, or until most of the excess liquid has evaporated. Taste and adjust seasoning, adding more chili if slightly hotter flavor is liked.

5 Just before serving, cut the avocado in half lengthwise and discard the pit. Cut into quarters lengthwise and peel away the skin, then cut the flesh into neat thin slices lengthwise. Brush with the lemon juice to prevent discoloration.

6 Stir the cheese into the beef until just beginning to melt, then spoon the mixture into a warmed serving dish and arrange the avocado slices around the edge. Serve at once.

Cook's Notes

TIME
Preparation 30 minutes, cooking 45 minutes.

BUYING GUIDE
Various grades of ground beef are available, but for this dish choose a good-quality, lean beef and use it on the day of purchase.

Cheaper grades of ground beef will require longer cooking and any excess fat should be skimmed from the top before serving.

VARIATION
If you do not have any chili seasoning (available in jars from most supermarkets), use the same quantity of mild curry powder; this will season the beef, but will not be sufficient to give a strong curry flavor. Chili powder can be used, but as it is hotter than chili seasoning, add a little at a time to the required strength.

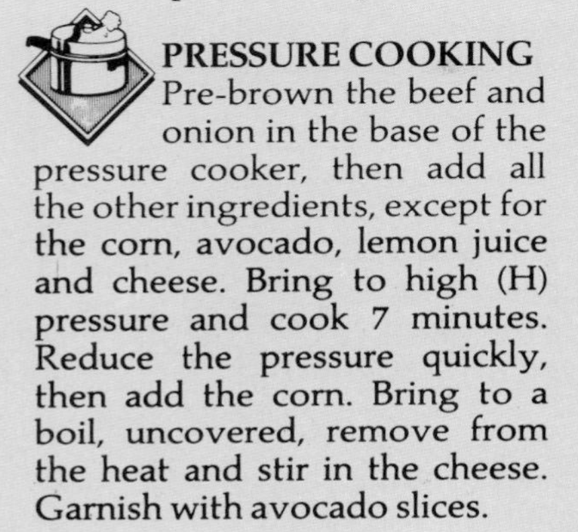

PRESSURE COOKING
Pre-brown the beef and onion in the base of the pressure cooker, then add all the other ingredients, except for the corn, avocado, lemon juice and cheese. Bring to high (H) pressure and cook 7 minutes. Reduce the pressure quickly, then add the corn. Bring to a boil, uncovered, remove from the heat and stir in the cheese. Garnish with avocado slices.

•555 calories per portion

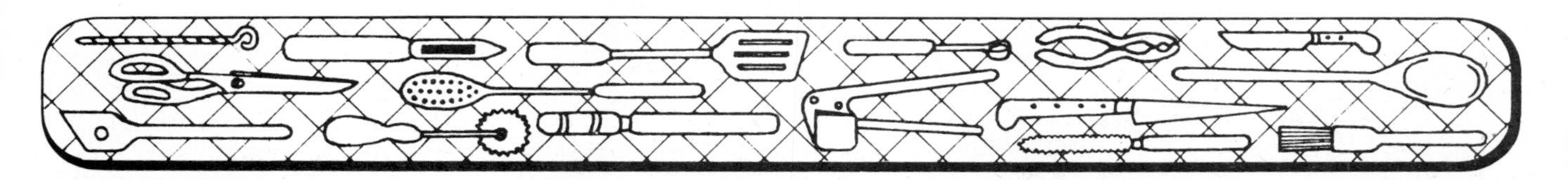

Beef curry

SERVES 4

1½ lb stewing steak, trimmed of excess fat and cut into ½-inch cubes
1 teaspoon ground coriander
1 teaspoon ground turmeric
1 teaspoon chili powder
½ teaspoon ground ginger
2 tablespoons vegetable oil
1 onion, sliced
1 clove garlic, crushed (optional)
1½ cups beef broth
1 tablespoon shredded coconut
1 tablespoon lemon juice
salt

1 Put the coriander, turmeric, chili and ginger in a bowl and gradually add a little water, stirring all the time until a smooth paste is formed. Set aside.

2 Heat the oil in a large flameproof casserole, add the onion and garlic, if using, and cook for 5 minutes until the onion is soft and lightly colored.

3 Stir in the spicy paste and cook a further 3-4 minutes, stirring all the time.

4 Add the meat and cook a further 3-4 minutes, stirring to cook on all sides in the spices. Stir in the broth and bring to a boil, then lower the heat and stir in the coconut, lemon juice and salt to taste. Cover and simmer gently 2 hours  until the meat is tender.

5 Taste and adjust seasoning (see Cook's tips) then serve hot, straight from the casserole.

Cook's Notes

TIME
15 minutes initial preparation, then 2 hours cooking time.

COOK'S TIPS
All curries have an infinitely better flavor if left to go cold overnight and are reheated the following day.

For extra "bite", add more lemon juice before serving.

● 405 calories per portion

Stir-fried beef with cashews

SERVES 4

1 lb rump steak or flash-fry steak, cut ½ inch thick and all fat removed (see Cook's tip)
3 tablespoons vegetable oil
1 clove garlic, crushed (optional)
4 scallions, cut into 1-inch pieces
1 large onion, chopped
½ cup unsalted cashew nuts
1 small green or red pepper, seeded and cut into thin strips
1 teaspoon ground ginger
1 tablespoon cornstarch
⅔ cup chicken broth
2 teaspoons medium sherry
2 teaspoons soy sauce
salt and freshly ground black pepper

1 Dry the beef on paper towels. Place it between 2 sheets of waxed paper and beat to flatten, with a wooden rolling pin. Using kitchen scissors, snip the beef into thin strips about 2 inches long.
2 Heat 1 tablespoon of oil in a large skillet or wok, add half the beef strips, stir about 1 minute until browned on all sides, [!] remove from the pan with a slotted spoon and reserve. Heat 1 more tablespoon of oil in the pan, add the remaining beef strips, stir-fry in the same way and reserve.
3 Heat the remaining oil in the pan add the garlic, if using, scallions, onion, cashew nuts and pepper strips and cook gently 3-4 minutes, stirring, until the vegetables are tender and the nuts lightly browned. Remove the pan from the heat and stir in the ginger.
4 Blend the cornstarch with the chicken broth, sherry and soy sauce to make a smooth paste, and stir into the pan.
5 Return to the heat, bring to a boil, lower heat and simmer gently 1 minute, stirring constantly. Season to taste with salt and pepper.
6 Return the reserved cooked beef strips to the pan and stir over gentle heat until heated through. Serve at once in individual bowls.

Cook's Notes

TIME
Preparation and cooking take about 30 minutes.

SERVING IDEAS
Serve with fine Chinese egg noodles, and chopped spinach.

VARIATIONS
Add walnut halves or use halved, blanched almonds instead of cashew nuts.

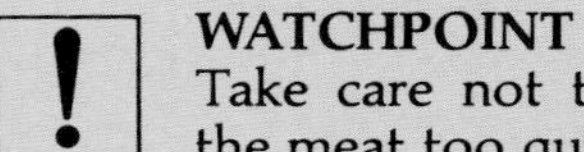

WATCHPOINT
Take care not to cook the meat too quickly or too long at this stage or it may toughen.

COOK'S TIP
The beef must be cut thinly: No thicker than ½ inch.

● 370 calories per portion

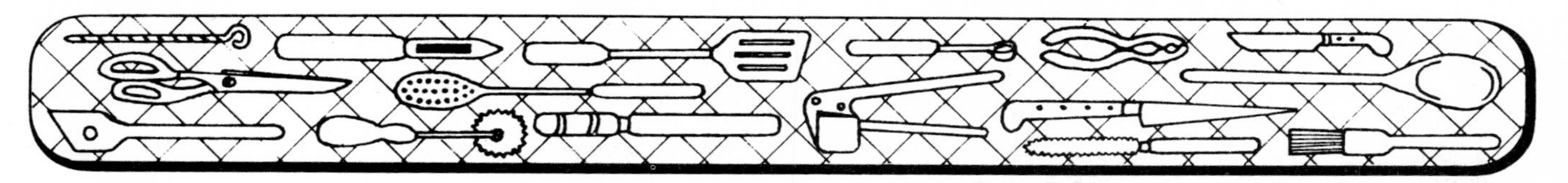

Beef goulash

SERVES 4

1 lb chuck steak, cubed
½ lb stewing veal, cubed
2 tablespoons butter or margarine
2 tablespoons vegetable oil
2 large onions, finely chopped
2 teaspoons paprika
1 can (about 14 oz) tomatoes, drained
⅓ lb button mushrooms
¼ cup beef broth or water
1 tablespoon tomato paste
salt and freshly ground black pepper
⅔ cup dairy sour cream
1 tablespoon chopped parsley

1 Preheat the oven to 325°.

2 Heat the butter and half the oil in a skillet, add the onions and cook without browning over low heat. Drain and remove to a casserole.

3 Add the remaining oil to the pan and cook the meat over high heat until evenly browned. Sprinkle the paprika over, cook 1-2 minutes and remove to the casserole.

4 Chop the tomatoes, lay them on top of the meat, and add the whole mushrooms, broth and tomato paste. Season with salt and pepper. Cover and cook in the oven, until the meat is tender about 2-2½ hours. Taste and adjust seasoning. ✳ Before serving, stir in half the sour cream and pour the rest over the top. Sprinkle with chopped parsley. Serve at once.

Cook's Notes

TIME
Preparation will take 25-30 minutes. Cook the goulash 2-2½ hours, until the meat is tender when tested with a fork.

• 530 calories per portion

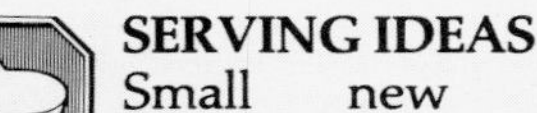

SERVING IDEAS
Small new boiled potatoes are nicest with goulash, but you can also serve mashed potatoes, macaroni or noodles with a crisp green vegetable such as broccoli or green beans.

FREEZING
Freeze in casserole. Tip out, wrap in foil, and replace in freezer. When ready to use, turn back into the casserole which was used for cooking. Cover and reheat until the goulash is bubbling.

Serbian beef

SERVES 4

2 lb stewing beef, trimmed and cut into bite-sized pieces
2 tablespoons vegetable oil
2 large onions, sliced
1 tablespoon paprika
1 celery stalk, chopped
2 cloves garlic, crushed (optional)
1 bay leaf
1 tablespoon chopped parsley
salt and freshly ground black pepper
⅔ cup red wine vinegar (see Cook's tip)
4 potatoes, thinly sliced
vegetable oil, for brushing

1 Preheat the oven to 300° and lightly brush a large ovenproof dish with oil.

2 Heat half the oil in a heavy flameproof casserole over high heat and cook the meat in batches, if necessary, until crisp and golden on all sides. Transfer the meat with a slotted spoon to a plate.

3 Add the remaining oil to the pan and cook the onions gently about 5 minutes until soft and translucent.

4 Return the meat and any juices to the pan. Add the paprika and stir over low heat for 2 minutes.

5 Add the celery, garlic, if using, bay leaf, parsley, salt and pepper to taste and the wine vinegar. Bring to a boil, remove from the heat and then allow to cool down for a few minutes.

6 Put half the potatoes in a layer on the bottom of the oiled ovenproof dish, cover with the meat mixture and then add the remaining potatoes in a neat layer on top. Cover tightly with a top or foil and cook in the oven about 2½ hours until the meat is tender.

7 Brush the potatoes with oil and place the casserole under a high broiler 5 minutes until the potatoes are browned. Serve hot straight from the dish.

Cook's Notes

TIME
Preparation takes 30 minutes; cooking 2½ hours.

VARIATIONS
Use other vegetables such as leeks and carrots, thinly sliced, with the celery.

COOK'S TIP
Wine vinegar helps tenderize the beef and adds a pleasant piquancy to the dish.

DID YOU KNOW
As its name suggests, this dish is traditional in Eastern Europe. It provides a hearty meal, particularly welcome in cold weather.

• 645 calories per portion

Apple-stuffed veal chops

SERVES 4

4 veal chops, each weighing about ½ lb, trimmed of excess fat (see Buying guide)
2 large green apples
juice of ½ lemon
2 tablespoons golden raisins
1½ teaspoons ground cloves
salt and freshly ground black pepper
1 tablespoon vegetable oil
2 tablespoons butter or margarine
2 tablespoons golden raisins, soaked in 1 tablespoon sherry, to garnish

1 Using a very sharp knife, make a pocket in each chop: Slit horizontally, from the outside edge to the bone, cutting through to within ½ inch of the edge.
2 Quarter, pare and core 1 apple. Cut into ¼-inch slices and put into a bowl with the lemon juice. Toss the apple slices in the lemon juice, then add the golden raisins and 1 teaspoon of ground cloves. Mix together well.
3 Spoon the apple mixture into the pocket of each chop, dividing it equally between them. Secure the slit edges with wooden toothpicks. Sprinkle the chops with the remaining ground cloves and season well with salt and freshly ground black pepper.
4 Heat the oil and butter in a large skillet, add the veal chops and cook them over high heat 2-3 minutes on each side, to brown and seal. Lower the heat and cook 10-15 minutes on each side, until cooked through and the juices run clear when the meat is pierced.
5 Pare and core the remaining apple. Slice into rings. Using a turner transfer chops to a warmed serving platter and keep warm. Add the apple rings to the skillet and cook gently, turning carefully so that the rings do not break up, until golden brown.
6 Arrange the cooked apple rings on top of the chops, spoon the golden raisins into the center of the apple rings and serve the apple-stuffed veal chops at once (see Serving ideas).

Cook's Notes

TIME
Preparing and cooking the veal chops takes only 30 minutes.

BUYING GUIDE
Veal chops are cut from the loin. As the loin is usually sold in one piece for roasting, veal chops may have to be ordered in advance from the butcher.

ECONOMY
Use 4 thick pork chops, in place of the veal chops used here.

SERVING IDEAS
Serve the veal chops with an apple juice sauce, if liked. Pour off excess fat from the skillet after cooking the apples. Pour in ⅔ cup apple juice, then bring slowly to a boil, stirring and scraping the sediment from the bottom of the pan with a wooden spoon. Remove from the heat and stir in 3 tablespoons heavy cream. Season to taste with salt and pepper. Spoon the sauce over the apples and veal to serve.

● 305 calories per portion

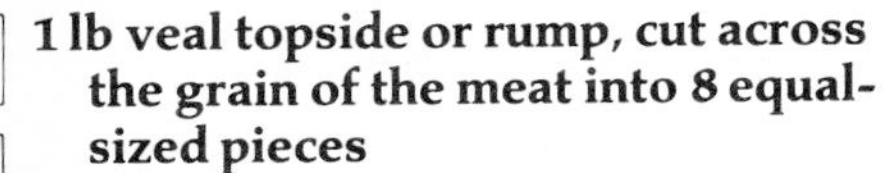

Italian veal rolls

SERVES 4

1 lb veal topside or rump, cut across the grain of the meat into 8 equal-sized pieces
4 thin square slices cooked ham, halved
1 tablespoon Dijon-style mustard (optional)
¼ lb Edam or Gouda cheese cut into 8 sticks 2 × ½ inch (see Watchpoint)
2 tablespoons butter
2 tablespoons vegetable oil
1 onion, chopped
1 clove garlic, crushed (optional)
¼ lb mushrooms sliced
1 can, (about 14 oz) tomatoes, drained and chopped
⅓ cup chicken broth
½ teaspoon dried oregano
1 bay leaf
salt and freshly ground black pepper
chopped chives, to garnish

1 Place the veal pieces between 2 sheets of waxed paper and pound with a wooden rolling pin or mallet, to flatten to the same size as the halved ham slices. Spread the ham slices with the mustard, if using.

2 Place a slice of ham on each piece of veal, mustard side down if used. Place a cheese stick at one end, then roll the veal and ham up around the cheese. Tie the rolls at both ends with fine string (see Preparation).

3 Heat the butter with the oil in a large skillet. When sizzling, add the veal rolls and cook over moderate heat about 6 minutes to brown on all sides. Remove the rolls from the pan with a slotted spoon or kitchen tongs and leave to drain on paper towels.

4 Add the onion and garlic, if using, to the pan and cook 5 minutes over gentle heat until soft and lightly colored. Add the mushrooms to the pan and cook a further 3 minutes.

5 Stir the tomatoes, broth and oregano into the pan, add the bay leaf and season to taste with salt and pepper. Bring to a boil. Return the veal rolls to the pan and turn in the sauce.

6 Lower the heat, cover the pan and cook gently 10 minutes. Uncover and cook a further 10 minutes or until the veal is tender and the sauce has reduced by about one-half.

7 Remove the rolls from the pan and carefully remove the string. Place the rolls in a warmed serving dish and keep hot. Discard the bay leaf from the sauce and taste and adjust seasoning.

8 Spoon the sauce over the veal rolls and sprinkle with chives. Serve.

Cook's Notes

TIME
Preparation takes about 45 minutes, cooking 35-40 minutes.

PREPARATION
Make the veal rolls in the following way:

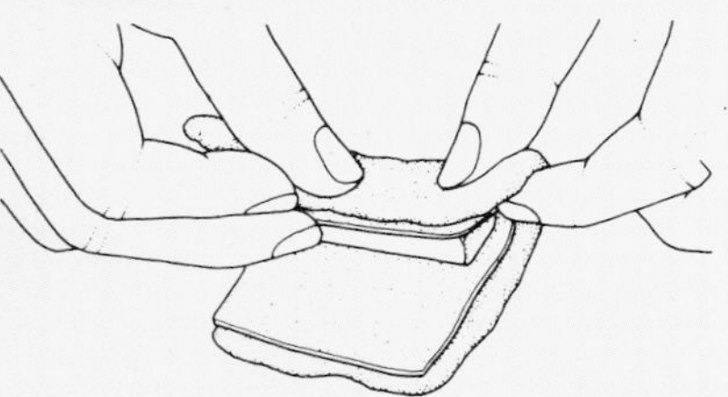

1 *Place the cheese stick at one end of the ham and roll up.*

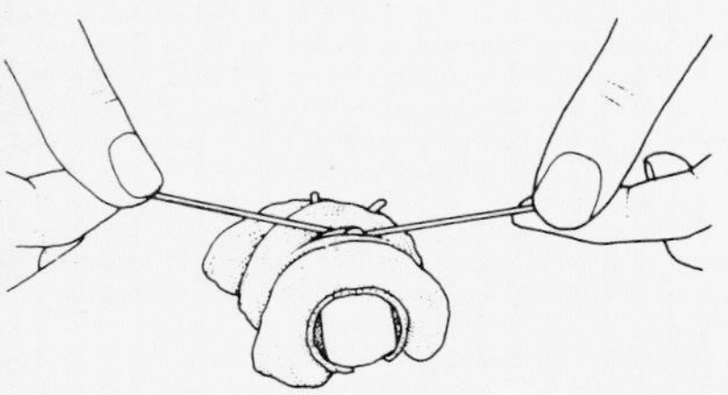

2 *Tie the rolls at either end with fine string as shown.*

WATCHPOINT
The cheese sticks must not protrude from the ends of the rolls, or the cheese will ooze out during cooking.

SPECIAL OCCASION
Use Swiss cheese, Parma ham, and dry white wine or vermouth instead of chicken broth.

• 415 calories per portion

Ratatouille veal

SERVES 4

3-3½ lb boned breast of veal (boned weight)
1 teaspoon chopped fresh basil or ½ teaspoon dried basil
¼ cup vegetable oil

RATATOUILLE STUFFING

3 tablespoons olive oil
1 onion finely chopped
1 eggplant, weighing about ½ lb, peeled and cut into ½-inch cubes, salted, drained, rinsed and dried
1 small green pepper, seeded and finely chopped
2 large tomatoes, peeled and chopped
1 teaspoon chopped fresh basil or ½ teaspoon dried basil
salt and freshly ground black pepper

1 Make the stuffing: Heat the oil in a saucepan, add the onion and cook gently 5 minutes until soft and lightly colored. Add the remaining stuffing ingredients with salt and pepper to taste and cook gently 15 minutes, stirring from time to time. Remove the stuffing from the heat and leave to cool.

2 Preheat the oven to 375°.

3 Pat the veal dry with paper towels. With a very sharp knife make a pocket in the veal by slitting horizontally through one long edge to within 1 inch of other 3 edges. Spoon the cooled ratatouille into the pocket (see Preparation). Using a trussing needle and fine string, sew up the opening (see Preparation).

4 Place the ratatouille-stuffed veal in a roasting pan. Sprinkle with the basil, season with salt and pepper and brush with the oil. Cover the veal with foil and then roast in the oven ¾ hour, basting often. Remove foil and roast a further ¾ hour, basting often, until the veal is tender (the juices run clear when the meat is pierced with a fine skewer).

5 Remove from oven and cut away trussing string. Transfer veal to a warmed serving dish and serve at once, cut into slices.

Cook's Notes

TIME
Preparation takes about 30 minutes, cooking about 1½ hours.

PREPARATION
To stuff the veal with ratatouille:

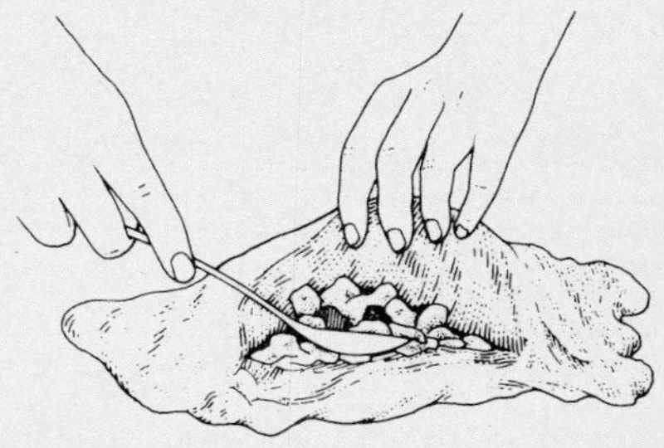

Spoon the ratatouille into the pocket, packing it in well.

Sew up the opening in the veal with trussing thread.

SERVING IDEAS
This tasty and unusual dish may be accompanied with croquette potatoes and, if liked, a green salad.

● 760 calories per portion

Veal with Stilton and walnuts

SERVES 4-6

3-3½ lb boned shoulder of veal
1 tablespoon vegetable oil
1 tablespoon butter
2 cups chicken broth
bouquet garni
⅓ lb mushrooms, sliced
2 teaspoons cornstarch
2 teaspoons water
walnut halves, to garnish

STUFFING

¼ lb Stilton cheese
½ cup shelled walnuts, chopped
3 tablespoons parsley and thyme package stuffing mix
salt and freshly ground black pepper
1 egg
2 tablespoons water

1 Preheat the oven to 350°.

2 Make the stuffing: Put the Stilton into a bowl and mash it with a fork. Stir in the walnuts and the stuffing mix. Season with salt and pepper. Beat the egg with the water and stir into the mixture.

3 Lay the veal skin side down on a board or work surface. Spread the stuffing mixture over it. Roll the veal up from one short end, then tie securely with string in several places to neaten the roll.

4 Heat the oil and butter in a large flameproof casserole. Add the veal and cook over brisk heat, turning, to brown and seal the meat. Drain any excess fat from the casserole and pour the broth around the veal. Add the bouquet garni. Cover with foil, then with the top and cook in the oven 1 hour (see Cook's tip).

5 Add the mushrooms to the casserole, cover again with the foil and top and cook a further 30 minutes, or until the veal is cooked through and the juices run clear when the meat is pierced with a skewer.

6 Place the veal on a warmed serving dish and remove the string. Keep the veal warm in the oven turned to its lowest setting while making the sauce.

7 Transfer the casserole to the top of the range and bring the cooking liquid to a boil. Blend the cornstarch to a smooth paste with the water in a small bowl, stir in a little of the hot cooking liquid, then stir this mixture back into the casserole. Cook, stirring, 1-2 minutes until the sauce thickens, then taste and adjust seasoning.

8 Carve veal into neat slices, then garnish with walnuts. Pour over a little sauce and pass the rest separately in a warmed gravyboat.

Cook's Notes

TIME

Preparation takes about 20 minutes. Cooking in the oven takes 1½ hours, making the sauce takes only about 5 minutes.

COOK'S TIP

Veal is best braised in liquid rather than dry roasted: Braising helps prevent the meat, on which there is little fat, from becoming dry.

● 703 calories per portion

Pot-roasted leg of lamb

SERVES 4-6

3 lb leg of lamb (see Buying guide)
⅔ cup red wine
⅔ cup water
1 tablespoon white wine vinegar
1 medium onion, finely chopped
1 teaspoon dried oregano
2 tablespoons vegetable oil
2 tablespoons tomato paste
pinch of sugar
salt and freshly ground black pepper
chopped parsley, to garnish

1 Put the lamb into a large bowl. Mix together the wine, water, vinegar, onion and oregano and pour over the lamb. Cover and leave to marinate in the refrigerator several hours, preferably overnight. Turn the lamb in the marinade from time to time.

2 Remove the lamb and reserve the marinade. Pat the lamb all over with paper towels until dry.

3 Heat the oil in a large flameproof casserole, add the lamb and cook over moderate heat until browned on all sides. Pour over the reserved marinade and cover the casserole with a tight fitting top. Cook over low heat 1½-2 hours or until the meat is cooked to your liking.

4 Remove the lamb and keep hot. Skim off any fat from the cooking liquid with a slotted spoon, then stir in the tomato paste and sugar. Bring to a boil, add salt and pepper to taste, then lower the heat and return the lamb to the casserole. Simmer gently a further 5 minutes.

5 To serve: Transfer the lamb to a warmed serving dish, pour over the sauce and sprinkle with parsley. Serve at once.

Cook's Notes

TIME
Preparation takes only a few minutes, but the lamb needs several hours to marinate. Cooking time is 1½-2 hours.

SERVING IDEAS
A pot roast makes a welcome, often more succulent, change to the traditional roast meal on a Sunday, but it can still be served with all the traditional accompaniments to a roast.

BUYING GUIDE
Ask for the chump end of a large leg of lamb. Not only is it the meatiest part of the leg, it is also neater in shape and therefore easier to fit into a casserole dish.

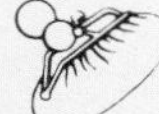

ECONOMY
For a more economical dish, use 1¼ cups well-flavored broth instead of the wine and water.

● 655 calories per portion

Breast of lamb and apple rounds

SERVES 4

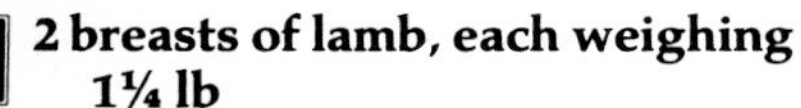

2 breasts of lamb, each weighing 1¼ lb
1 small onion, halved
1 small carrot, roughly chopped
1 celery stalk, roughly chopped
1 tablespoon chopped celery leaves (optional)
1 teaspoon whole cloves
3-inch piece stick cinnamon
2 bay leaves
1 sprig each fresh rosemary and thyme or pinch each dried rosemary and thyme
2 tablespoons cider vinegar or white wine vinegar
1 teaspoon black peppercorns
1 teaspoon salt

APPLE FILLING
2 large green apples, pared, cored and chopped
6 tablespoons cider vinegar
4 whole cloves

1 Put the vegetables, spices, herbs and vinegar in a large saucepan with the peppercorns and salt. Pour in enough water to cover the lamb – but do not add the lamb at this stage. Bring to a boil, then lower the heat and simmer 10 minutes.
2 Add the lamb, cover the pan and bring back to a boil. Lower the heat and simmer 1½ hours or until the meat is tender.
3 Let the lamb cool in the liquid in the pan.
4 Meanwhile, make the apple filling: Put the apples into a saucepan with the vinegar and cloves. Cover and cook over low heat 15 minutes or until the apple is very soft. Remove the cloves and, using a wooden spoon, mash the apples to a purée.
5 When the lamb is cool enough to handle, lift out of the liquid and remove the bones and as much of the skin and the fat as possible (see Preparation).
6 Spread the lamb breasts with the apple purée then roll them up and tie with kitchen string. Leave in a cool place at least 4 hours to set into shape.
7 Preheat the broiler to high.
8 Bring the breasts of lamb to room temperature, then cut each roll into 4 thick slices, leaving the string in place.
9 Broil the rounds of lamb until they are brown and crisp on both sides (10-15 minutes in all). Remove the string and serve at once.

Cook's Notes

TIME
Preparation and cooking time 3¾ hours, but allow 4 hours for the lamb to cool before slicing.

PREPARATION
A way to bone and skin the breast of lamb is shown below:

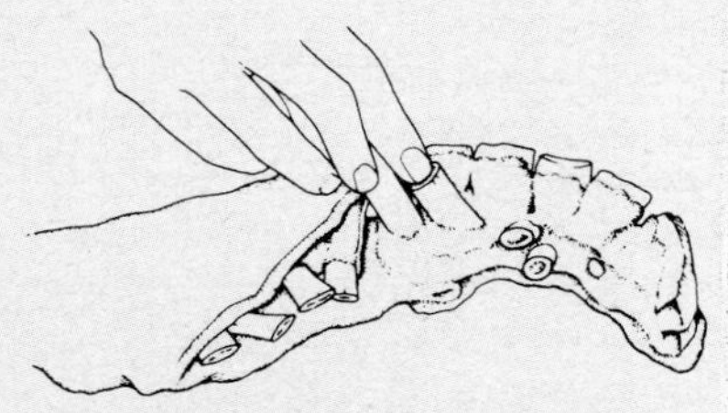

1 *Once the lamb has been boiled, the bones pull out easily.*

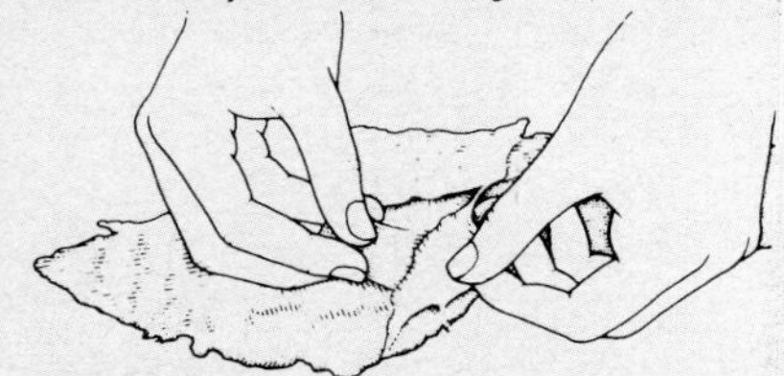

2 *To remove the piece of cartilage between the layers, gently ease the meat apart and pull it away.*

● 545 calories per portion

Lamb chops and peppers

SERVES 4
- 4 large loin lamb chops, trimmed
- 4 tablespoons vegetable oil
- 2 medium onions, thinly sliced
- 1 clove garlic, chopped (optional)
- 1 lb tomatoes, peeled, seeded and chopped
- 2 green peppers, seeded and cut into strips
- 1 red pepper, seeded and cut into strips
- 1 teaspoon crushed coriander seeds (optional)
- salt and freshly ground black pepper
- ⅔ cup dry white wine
- 1 tablespoon tomato paste

1 Heat the oil in a large skillet over high heat. Brown the chops on both sides, cooking in 2 batches if necessary.

2 With all the chops in the pan, lower the heat, put in onions and garlic, if using, and cover pan. Cook about 10 minutes until the onions and garlic are soft and beginning to color.

3 Add the tomatoes, peppers, coriander and salt and pepper to taste. Cover the pan again and cook a further 15 minutes or until the chops are tender.

4 Remove chops from pan and keep hot. Raise the heat and stir the wine into the pan. Cook rapidly, uncovered, until the liquid in the pan is reduced by half, stirring the sauce constantly.

5 Stir in the tomato paste and simmer, uncovered, 5 minutes. Taste and adjust seasoning.

6 Place the chops on a warmed serving platter, then spoon the sauce over them. Serve at once.

Cook's Notes

TIME
Preparation 15 minutes, cooking 40-45 minutes.

FREEZING
After cooking is completed, place in a suitable container, seal, label and freeze. Store up to 6 months. To serve: Thaw or reheat from frozen until thoroughly heated through. Add a little extra water or wine if the sauce has too thick a consistency.

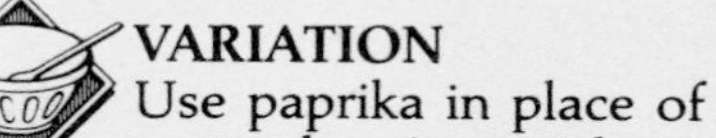

VARIATION
Use paprika in place of coriander. A can (about 14 oz) of tomatoes may be substituted for fresh.

• 490 calories per portion

Roast lamb with zucchini sauce

SERVES 4

½ shoulder lamb, weighing about 2 lb
1 clove garlic (optional), cut into thin slices
grated rind of ½ lemon
1½ teaspoons clear honey

SAUCE
2 tablespoons butter or margarine
1 small onion, finely chopped
½ lb zucchini, grated
juice of ½ lemon
1¼ cups chicken broth
1 teaspoon superfine sugar
salt and freshly ground black pepper

1 Preheat the oven to 400°.
2 Place the lamb in a roasting pan skin side up. Score the surface with a sharp knife to make a trellis pattern. Make a series of small slits within the trellis squares; press a garlic sliver, if using, into each.
3 Sprinkle the surface of the lamb with the lemon rind, then spread thinly with the honey.
4 Roast the lamb about 1¼ hours (see Cook's tip), until the juices run clear when the thickest part of the meat is pierced with a sharp knife or skewer.
5 Meanwhile, make the sauce: Melt the butter in a skillet, add the onion and cook gently about 5 minutes until soft and lightly colored. Stir in the grated zucchini, and cook stirring for a further 2-3 minutes, then stir in the lemon juice and broth. Bring the sauce slowly to a boil, add the sugar and season to taste with salt and pepper. Remove from the heat and leave to cool slightly, then pour into a blender and work to a smooth purée. Reheat gently, if necessary, to serve.
6 Remove the lamb from the oven and transfer to a warmed serving platter. Carve a few slices and pour over a little of the sauce. Serve at once, with the remaining sauce passed separately in a warmed gravyboat.

Cook's Notes

TIME
Preparing the lamb and making the sauce takes 30 minutes. Roasting in the oven takes about 1¼ hours.

COOK'S TIP
The total cooking time for shoulder of lamb is calculated at 25 minutes per 1 lb, plus 25 minutes.

BUYING GUIDE
Choose the blade joint half of the shoulder: It is meatier than the knuckle.

PRESSURE COOKING
Make sure the lamb fits comfortably in the cooker and that there is enough headroom. Pre-brown the lamb in hot fat, then drain. Put the trivet into the base of the cooker, place the lamb on it and pour in 1¼ cups broth. Cook at high (H) pressure 24 minutes. Release pressure quickly. Crisp the lamb in a 400° oven 10-12 minutes, while making the sauce.

● 470 calories per portion

Egg and almond lamb

SERVES 4
1 lb boneless lean lamb, ground (see Economy)
4 slices white bread, torn into pieces
1¼ cups milk
1 tablespoon vegetable oil
1 large onion, finely chopped
2 teaspoons curry powder
2 teaspoons sugar
2 teaspoons lemon juice
⅓ cup packed golden raisins
½ teaspoon salt
2 eggs, beaten
¼ cup flaked almonds

1 Preheat the oven to 375°.
2 Put the bread into a bowl and pour over the milk. Leave to soak.
3 Meanwhile heat the oil in a large skillet, add the onion and cook gently until soft. Stir in the curry powder, sugar and lemon juice and cook 1-2 minutes, stirring.
4 Squeeze the milk from the bread, reserving the milk. Beat the bread with a fork to break it up.
5 Add the meat and bread to the onion mixture and cook until the meat is well browned. Stir in the raisins and salt; remove from heat.
6 Add a quarter of the beaten eggs to meat mixture and pour into a greased ovenproof dish. Level the surface, then bake 30 minutes.
7 Meanwhile, beat the reserved milk into the remaining eggs.
8 Lower the oven heat to 350°. Drain away fat from the lamb, then pour over the egg mixture. Scatter the almonds on top and cook 30 minutes.

Cook's Notes

TIME
Preparation 30 minutes, cooking 1 hour.

ECONOMY
Shoulder of lamb is probably the most economical cut to use for this recipe, but you will have to trim it well before cooking or the finished dish may be too fatty. This recipe is also an excellent way to use up left-over lamb from the weekend roast. Grind or chop it finely, then follow the method above, omitting the initial 30 minutes baking.

DID YOU KNOW
Almonds are one of the world's most popular nuts. They are often mentioned in the Old Testament and were known by the Romans as "the Greek nut". They were also eaten before meals in medieval times, in the belief this would prevent drunkenness.

SERVING IDEAS
As this is a substantial dish on its own, it needs nothing more than a seasonal vegetable or salad.

● 620 calories per portion

Indian skewered lamb

SERVES 4

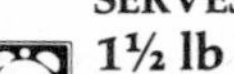

1½ lb lean lamb (preferably cut from the fillet or top end of the leg) cut into 1-inch cubes, trimmed of excess fat
1¼ cups plain yogurt
1 onion, finely grated
1 teaspoon ground ginger
2 tablespoons garam masala (see Buying guide)
½ teaspoon chili powder
salt
1 large green pepper, seeded and cut into 1 inch-squares
1 large red pepper, seeded and cut into 1 inch-squares
24 button mushrooms, trimmed
vegetable oil, for greasing

1 In large bowl, mix together the yogurt, onion, ginger, garam masala, chili powder and salt to taste. Add the cubes of lamb to the mixture, turning them over so that each piece is well-coated. Cover with plastic wrap and leave to marinate in a cool place (not in the refrigerator) overnight.

2 Preheat the oven to 375°.

3 Remove the lamb from the marinade but do not wipe off the yogurt coating. Thread the meat, the red and green peppers and mushrooms alternately onto 8 oiled kabob skewers.

4 Brush the inside of a large roasting pan with oil and place the skewers in it side-by-side (see Cook's tips). Brush the meat with a little oil, then cook in the oven about 1 hour, until the meat is tender, turning the skewers and brushing them with more oil every 15 minutes. Transfer the skewers to a bed of plain rice and serve at once, with the tasty juices from the roasting pan spooned carefully over the kabobs.

Cook's Notes

TIME
10 minutes initial preparation, then overnight marinating. To prepare ingredients and thread skewers about 30 minutes, then about 1 hour cooking.

BUYING GUIDE
Garam masala – an aromatic spice mix – is available from Indian shops, supermarkets and delicatessens.

COOK'S TIPS
For this quantity of meat and vegetables, you will need skewers 10 inches long.

Alternatively, you can cook the kabobs for an outdoor meal over a barbecue.

● 365 calories per portion

Lamb and asparagus casserole

SERVES 4

2½ lb half shoulder of lamb, boned, excess fat removed, cut into 1-inch cubes (see Buying guide)
1 tablespoon all-purpose flour
1 tablespoon chopped fresh thyme, or 1 teaspoon dried thyme
salt and freshly ground black pepper
1 tablespoon vegetable oil
2 shallots, chopped
1 clove garlic, crushed (optional)
1¼ cups water
⅓ cup medium white wine
1 lb fresh or frozen asparagus (see Preparation)
¼ lb mushrooms, sliced
2 tablespoons heavy cream and asparagus spears, to finish

1 Preheat the oven to 325°.
2 Put the flour in a large plastic bag, add half the thyme and salt and pepper to taste. Add lamb cubes and shake to coat well. Reserve any excess seasoned flour.
3 Heat the oil in a large flameproof casserole, add the lamb cubes and cook quickly over brisk heat to brown and seal on all sides. Remove from the pan with a slotted spoon and leave to drain thoroughly on paper towels.
4 Add the shallots to the casserole with the garlic, if using, and cook gently 5 minutes until soft and lightly colored. Sprinkle in any excess seasoned flour, stir in the water and wine and season to taste with salt and pepper. Bring to a boil, then return the lamb cubes to the casserole ✳ and stir in the remaining thyme.
5 Cover and cook in the oven about 1½ hours.
6 Add the blanched asparagus and the mushrooms to the casserole and cook a further 30 minutes, until the lamb is cooked through and tender when pierced with a sharp knife. Swirl over the cream, garnish with asparagus spears. Serve at once, straight from the casserole.

Cook's Notes

TIME
Preparation 30 minutes, cooking 2 hours.

PREPARATION
Fresh asparagus needs to be blanched: Trim off woody bases of stems and cut stems into 2-3 inch lengths. Simmer 5 minutes in salted water, drain. Add frozen asparagus straight to casserole.

FREEZING
Cook the casserole in a foil container, cool quickly, then seal, label and freeze up to 3 months. To serve: Thaw overnight in the refrigerator, then reheat in a 350° oven 30-40 minutes until bubbling.

BUYING GUIDE
Half shoulder of lamb is an economical cut, very suitable for casseroles.

The asparagus season is short, so it is worth making the most of it while home-grown asparagus is least expensive. Choose thick-stemmed asparagus, usually sold in bundles, for this recipe: The less expensive, thin-stemmed asparagus is unsuitable.

● 590 calories per portion

Lamb ratatouille

SERVES 4

4 large loin or sirloin lamb chops, trimmed of fat
3 tablespoons olive or corn oil
1 onion roughly chopped
1 can (about 12 oz) tomatoes, peeled and roughly chopped
1 eggplant, peeled, cut into 1-inch cubes
2 zucchini, cut into 1-inch slices
1 green pepper, seeded and chopped
1-2 garlic cloves, crushed with ½ teaspoon salt
1 teaspoon dried basil
salt and freshly ground black pepper

1 Heat the oil in a heavy-based deep saucepan, add the onion and cook gently about 5 minutes until soft and lightly colored.

2 Stir in the tomatoes, then the eggplant, the zucchini, green pepper, garlic and basil. Bring the mixture to a boil, then lower the heat, cover and simmer about 30 minutes until the eggplant cubes are soft when pressed with a spoon. Stir the mixture frequently during this time.

3 Preheat the broiler to high.

4 Uncover the pan of ratatouille, increase the heat and boil rapidly until most of the liquid has evaporated. Taste and season with salt and pepper, then cover the pan again and keep the ratatouille warm on the lowest possible flame, stirring occasionally.

5 Lay the chops on the hot broiler rack and broil about 7 minutes on each side until browned and cooked through.

6 Spoon half the ratatouille into a warmed serving dish, arrange the chops in a single layer on top, then top each with a spoonful of the remaining ratatouille. Serve at once.

Cook's Notes

TIME
1 hour to prepare and cook the dish.

DID YOU KNOW
Ratatouille is best described as a French vegetable stew. Native to Provence in the south of France, it is made there with the best of the summer vegetables – eggplant, zucchini, peppers, tomatoes, onions and garlic.

SERVING IDEAS
Serve with spaghetti, pasta shells or spirals, or boiled or steamed rice.

FREEZING
Ratatouille freezes very successfully, and is a useful vegetable dish to keep in the freezer to serve with any roast or broiled meats. Transfer to a rigid container, cool quickly, then seal, label and store in the freezer up to 3 months. To serve: Reheat from frozen in a heavy-based saucepan, stirring frequently until bubbling. Take care not to overcook the vegetables or they will be mushy. Taste and adjust seasoning before serving.

• 750 calories per portion

Lamb with plums

SERVES 4

2½ lb lamb rib rack of lamb in one piece, boned (see Buying guide)
1 lb dark cooking plums
1 tablespoon butter or margarine
1 small onion, finely chopped
1 tablespoon chopped fresh parsley
2 teaspoons dried mixed herbs
⅔ cup whole wheat bread crumbs
2 tablespoons hot chicken broth
salt and freshly ground black pepper

SAUCE

1 tablespoon butter or margarine
1 small onion, finely chopped
2 teaspoons all-purpose flour
1¼ cups hot chicken broth
bouquet garni
4 tablespoons dry white wine
few drops of red food coloring (optional)

1 Preheat the oven to 350°.

2 Make a slit across the width of the thick end of the lamb, to make a pocket for the stuffing. Make the slit about 1½ inches deep, but do not cut right through.

3 Reserve 2 whole plums for the garnish. Pit and chop the rest.

4 To make the stuffing: Melt the butter in a small skillet, add the onion and cook gently 5 minutes until soft and lightly colored.

5 Remove the pan from the heat and stir in the parsley, herbs, bread crumbs and one-third of the chopped plums. Gradually add the broth and stir well. Season with salt and pepper to taste.

6 Place the lamb skin side down on a flat surface and spread the stuffing over it, and also push it into the slit. Roll the lamb and tie it with trussing thread or fine string in several places. Place the lamb in a roasting pan and roast in the oven 45 minutes.

7 Turn the lamb over and roast a further 45 minutes or until cooked to your liking. Meanwhile, make the sauce: Melt the butter in a small saucepan, add the onion and cook gently 5 minutes until soft and lightly colored. Sprinkle in the flour and stir over low heat 1-2 minutes. Gradually stir in the broth, bring to a boil, then add the remaining chopped plums, the bouquet garni and salt and pepper to taste. Lower the heat, cover and simmer 30 minutes, stirring occasionally.

8 Remove the bouquet garni from the sauce, then push the sauce through a strainer, pressing hard with a wooden spoon to extract as much liquid as possible. Set the sauce aside. Halve, pit and slice the 2 remaining plums.

9 When the lamb is cooked, lift it out of the roasting pan and keep hot with any loose stuffing from the pan.

10 Pour off all the fat from the roasting pan and place the pan on top of the stove. Pour in the wine and bring to a boil, scraping up all the sediment from the sides and bottom of the pan with a wooden spoon.

11 Stir in the sauce, lower the heat and simmer 1 minute, then strain to remove any black specks if necessary. If liked, stir in food coloring to make the sauce pink. Taste and adjust seasoning. Keep hot.

12 Carve the lamb into 8 thick slices and arrange on a warmed serving platter. Spoon a little sauce over each slice. Garnish with the sliced plums. Serve at once with the remaining sauce passed separately.

Cook's Notes

TIME
Preparation 35 minutes, cooking takes 1¾ hours.

BUYING GUIDE
Ask you butcher to bone the lamb for you.

• 560 calories per portion

Summer lamb

SERVES 4

½ leg of lamb, weighing about 2 lb (see Buying guide)
2 sprigs fresh rosemary
2 bay leaves
salt and freshly ground black pepper
2 tablespoons vegetable oil

TUNA MAYONNAISE

1 can (about 7 oz) tuna, drained and flaked
3 tablespoons thick mayonnaise
⅔ cup plain yogurt
2 teaspoons anchovy paste
grated rind of 1 lemon
1 tablespoon lemon juice

TO GARNISH

1 small red pepper, seeded and cut into strips
12 black olives

1 Preheat the oven to 375°.

2 Place the lamb on a large sheet of foil, and tuck the sprigs of rosemary and the bay leaves into the meat. Sprinkle with salt and pepper and brush with the oil. Wrap the foil around the meat and place in a roasting pan. Roast in the oven 1¼ hours or until the meat is tender (the juices run clear when the meat is pierced with a skewer).

3 Remove from the oven and leave the meat to cool overnight in its wrappings (see Cook's tips).

4 Make the tuna mayonnaise: Put the tuna in a blender with the mayonnaise, yogurt, anchovy paste, lemon rind and juice. Blend until the mixture is smooth. Alternatively, if you do not have a blender, mash the ingredients with a fork until well combined.

5 Pour into a bowl, then taste and add salt and pepper if necessary. Cover with plastic wrap and refrigerate until ready to serve.

6 Plunge the strips of pepper into boiling water 1 minute to blanch them, then drain and refresh under cold running water. Drain thoroughly.

7 Carve the cold lamb into thin slices. Lay the slices in a single layer on a serving dish and cover with the tuna mayonnaise (see Cook's tips). Arrange the strips of pepper in a lattice pattern over the mayonnaise and place the olives in the squares. Serve cold.

Cook's Notes

TIME
Cooking time for the lamb is 1¼ hours, but remember to allow it to cool overnight in a cold place.

Preparation of the tuna mayonnaise takes 10-15 minutes, and allow 10 minutes to finish.

COOK'S TIPS
You can use left-over lamb for this dish, but meat cooked and left to cool in the piece has a better flavor and is also more moist.

If the slices of lamb will not fit in the dish in a single layer, make 2 layers and separate them with a layer of half the mayonnaise mixture.

If you have any tuna mayonnaise left over it will make a delicious snack or appetizer served the following day spooned over halved hard-boiled eggs or a bed of shredded lettuce.

BUYING GUIDE
The frozen lamb joints sold in supermarkets are ideal for this recipe. If you are using frozen lamb make sure the joint is thoroughly thawed before cooking.

• 565 calories per portion

Lamb bake

SERVES 4

1 lb cooked lamb, cut into small cubes
¼ cup butter or margarine
1 tablespoon all-purpose flour
½ teaspoon dry mustard
1¼ cups canned beef consommé, undiluted
⅔ cup light cream
1 teaspoon Worcestershire sauce
2 hard-boiled eggs, quartered
¼ lb mushrooms, sliced
salt and freshly ground black pepper
½ cup fresh whole wheat bread crumbs
1 tablespoon chopped parsley

1 Preheat the oven to 350°.

2 Over low heat, gently melt half the butter in a flameproof casserole. Stir in the flour and mustard, mix well, raise the heat and cook about 1 minute, stirring constantly. Add the consommé and bring to a boil, stirring briskly. Continue to boil 2-3 minutes until sauce is cooked.

3 Lower the heat and add the cream, Worcestershire sauce, hard-boiled eggs, sliced mushrooms and the cooked lamb. Fold gently to mix, taking care not to break the eggs. Taste and adjust seasoning.

4 Melt the remaining butter in a separate pan and mix with the bread crumbs and parsley. Sprinkle on top of the casserole.

5 Bake uncovered in the heated oven about 30 minutes until the casserole is golden on top, and the meat heated through. Serve at once.

Cook's Notes

TIME
15 minutes preparation, 30 minutes cooking.

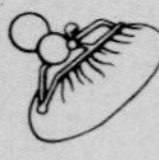

ECONOMY
This is an excellent way of using up leftover roast lamb.

SERVING IDEAS
Serve with golden brown sautéed potatoes (potatoes boiled until nearly cooked, then sliced and fried in hot oil), and a green vegetable.

VARIATIONS
Use 2-4 tablespoons red wine in place of some of the consommé for a richer flavor.

For a sharper taste, use plain yogurt in place of some or all of the light cream.

COOK'S TIP
To hard-boil eggs: Put eggs in a pan, cover with cold water and bring to a boil. Simmer 7-8 minutes only, then drain and immediately plunge into cold water. Remove shells and keep in cold water to prevent a black ring forming around yolks.

● 655 calories per portion

Spinach-stuffed lamb

SERVES 8

3-3½ lb shoulder of lamb, blade bone removed (see Buying guide)
all-purpose flour, for dusting
3 tablespoons vegetable oil

SPINACH STUFFING

¼ cup butter or margarine
1 onion, finely chopped
2 celery stalks, finely chopped
½ lb frozen chopped spinach
½ lb pork sausagemeat
1 egg, beaten
1 tablespoon finely chopped fresh mint, or 1 teaspoon dried mint
good pinch of freshly ground nutmeg
salt and freshly ground black pepper

1 Make the stuffing: Melt the butter in a saucepan, add the onion and celery and cook gently about 5 minutes until the vegetables are soft and lightly colored but not browned.

2 Meanwhile, cook the spinach in a separate pan about 4 minutes, stirring occasionally. Drain through a fine strainer, pressing with the back of a spoon to remove as much liquid from it as possible.

3 Mix the spinach into the cooked onion mixture and cook gently 1 minute, stirring constantly.

4 Mash the sausagemeat in a bowl. Add spinach mixture and stir well. Stir in the egg, mint and nutmeg. Season well with salt and pepper and mix thoroughly. Cover and refrigerate for 30 minutes.

5 Meanwhile preheat the oven to 325°.

6 With a sharp knife, carefully enlarge pocket left in the lamb by removal of the bone. Pack in prepared stuffing, pressing it down well. Draw edges of pocket together and secure with a meat skewer (see Cook's tip).

7 Cut a piece of foil nearly large enough to enclose the lamb. Line a roasting pan with the foil, then put the lamb, skin side up, in the pan. Season with salt and pepper and dust with flour. Pour the oil evenly over the surface of the lamb.

8 Bring the foil up closely around the sides of the lamb but do not cover the surface.

9 Roast the lamb in the oven 2 hours, basting occasionally with the juices in the foil.

10 Increase oven heat to 400°, open out foil and cook a further 30 minutes until the skin is crisp and browned and the meat is cooked through (the juices run clear when the lamb is pierced with a fine meat skewer).

11 Remove skewer and transfer lamb to a warmed carving dish. Return to oven turned to lowest setting 10-15 minutes for meat to "rest" so that it is easier to carve, then slice and serve.

Cook's Notes

TIME
Preparing the stuffing takes about 20 minutes, but allow 30 minutes chilling. Preparing the lamb for roasting takes about 15 minutes; cooking 2½ hours; 10-15 minutes for the meat to rest before carving.

BUYING GUIDE
Order the lamb in advance and ask your butcher to remove the blade bone. When stuffed in this way the shoulder should retain its shape.

COOK'S TIP
If the meat is firmly secured the stuffing should stay in place, but if a little does escape, use it as a garnish for the sliced lamb on the serving dish.

SERVING IDEAS
Serve with roast potatoes and buttered carrots to make an attractive color contrast with that of the spinach stuffing.

● 395 calories per portion

Chicken in lychee sauce

SERVES 4

3 chicken breasts, each weighing ⅓ lb, skinned
3 tablespoons cornstarch
3 tablespoons vegetable oil
1 onion, thinly sliced
1 chicken bouillon cube
2 tablespoons boiling water
2 tablespoons tomato catsup
2 teaspoons soy sauce
1 can (about 11 oz) lychees, drained and quartered, with syrup reserved
2 large tomatoes, peeled and roughly chopped
2 tablespoons chopped chives or chopped scallions
1-2 tablespoons lemon juice
freshly ground black pepper

1 Cut away any bones from the chicken with a sharp knife. Discard any fat. Cut the chicken into ½-inch cubes.

2 Put the cornstarch into a plastic bag then add the chicken cubes and shake until well coated.

3 Heat the oil in a large skillet, add the onion and cook gently 5 minutes until soft and lightly colored.

4 Raise the heat, add the chicken and cook about 5 minutes, turning frequently until lightly browned all over. Remove the pan from the heat.

5 In a bowl, dissolve the bouillon cube in the boiling water. Stir in the tomato catsup and soy sauce, then stir this mixture into the chicken together with the quartered lychees and reserved syrup, the tomatoes and half the chives. Mix well.

6 Return to the heat, bring to a boil, then simmer 1 minute, stirring constantly. Cover with a top or foil and simmer gently a further 5 minutes, or until the chicken is tender and cooked through. Stir in lemon juice and pepper to taste, then transfer to a warmed serving dish. Sprinkle with remaining chives. Serve at once.

Cook's Notes

TIME
40 minutes to prepare and cook.

SERVING IDEAS
Serve with fresh peas and fried, fresh beansprouts or boiled Chinese noodles.

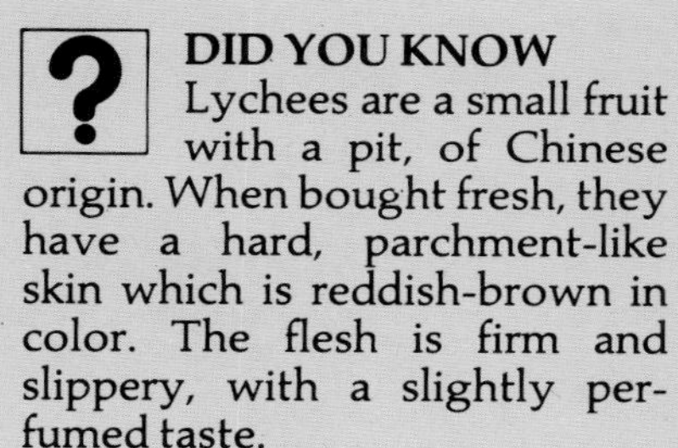

DID YOU KNOW
Lychees are a small fruit with a pit, of Chinese origin. When bought fresh, they have a hard, parchment-like skin which is reddish-brown in color. The flesh is firm and slippery, with a slightly perfumed taste.

VARIATION
Use a diced pepper instead of tomatoes.

PRESSURE COOKING
Without coating in cornstarch, pre-brown the chicken in the cooker, then add the rest of the ingredients, except for the lychees. Bring the pressure to high (H) and cook 5 minutes. Reduce the pressure quickly, add the cornstarch mixed with a little water, and simmer uncovered 2 minutes. Add lychees, heat through, stir in lemon juice.

● 325 calories per portion

Spanish stuffed chicken

SERVES 4-6

3-3½ lb roasting chicken
vegetable oil, for brushing

STUFFING
2 tablespoons butter or margarine
1 small onion, chopped
⅓ cup soft white bread crumbs
¼ cup blanched almonds, chopped
1 canned red pimiento, chopped
8 green olives, pitted and quartered
1 large tomato, peeled and chopped
½ teaspoon salt
freshly ground black pepper

1 Preheat the oven to 350°.
2 Make the stuffing: Melt the butter in a skillet, add the onion and cook gently 5 minutes until soft and lightly colored. Remove the pan from the heat.
3 Add the remaining stuffing ingredients to the pan and mix well.
4 Wash the chicken and pat dry with paper towels. Using a small sharp knife, remove the wishbone from the neck end of the chicken by cutting away the flesh around it (see Cook's tip). Break off the bone at the joints and lift it out.
5 Fill the neck cavity with the stuffing, fold the neck skin back into position, then fold the wing tips over it. Secure with a metal skewer. Carefully truss the drumsticks with string, if necessary.
6 Lightly oil a roasting pan. Place the chicken in the pan, brush with oil and season with salt and pepper.
7 Roast the chicken in the oven 1½ hours until cooked (the juices run clear when the thigh is pierced with a skewer). Remove skewer and any string and, if serving hot, transfer to a warmed serving dish (see Serving ideas).

Cook's Notes

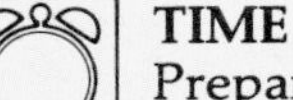

TIME
Preparation, including making the stuffing, takes about 30 minutes. Cooking takes about 1½ hours.

SERVING IDEAS
Make a gravy to serve with the hot chicken: Pour off most of the fat in the pan, leaving about 2 tablespoons of sediment. Stir in 2 teaspoons flour and cook over gentle heat 1-2 minutes, stirring constantly. Gradually blend in 1¼ cups hot chicken broth. Bring to a boil and cook 2-3 minutes. Taste and adjust seasoning if necessary. Strain into a warmed gravyboat.

COOK'S TIP
Removing the wishbone makes carving easier: The chicken can be sliced right down through the stuffing.

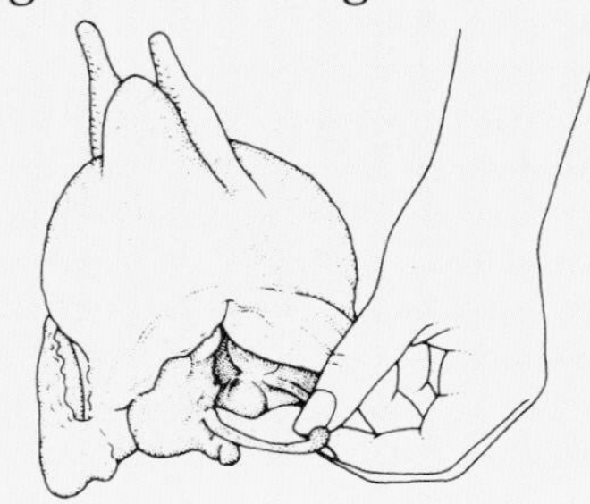

Cut away the flesh around the wishbone with a small sharp knife, then break at joints and remove.

• 525 calories per portion

Chicken curry

SERVES 4
4 chicken pieces, each weighing ¾ lb
2 tablespoons butter or margarine
2 onions, chopped
1 clove garlic, crushed (optional)
1 tablespoon all-purpose flour
1 tablespoon curry powder
3 tomatoes, peeled and roughly chopped
2 celery stalks, chopped
2 bananas, thickly sliced
1 dessert apple, roughly chopped
½ cup chicken broth
salt and freshly ground black pepper
1 cup yogurt or dairy sour cream
1½ tablespoons toasted flaked almonds, to garnish

1 Melt the butter in a large skillet and cook the chicken pieces over moderate heat until browned on both sides. Remove from the pan with a slotted spoon and set aside.

2 Add the onions to the pan with the garlic, if using, and cook 5 minutes until the onion is translucent. Stir in the flour and curry powder and cook 2-3 minutes, then stir in all the remaining ingredients except the salt, pepper and yogurt.

3 Bring to a boil, stirring constantly, then return the chicken pieces to the pan and season to taste with salt and pepper. Lower the heat, cover and cook gently about 45 minutes or until the chicken is tender when pierced with a skewer (see Cook's tips). ✱

4 Remove the chicken from the pan and keep hot on a serving plate. Boil the sauce until thick, then remove the pan from the heat and stir in the yogurt.

5 Taste and adjust seasoning (see Cook's tips), pour over the chicken and sprinkle with the flaked almonds. Serve at once.

Cook's Notes

TIME
The curry takes 20 minutes preparation plus 45 minutes cooking.

SERVING IDEAS
Serve with rice, chapati, or poppadoms and prepare separate bowls of mango chutney and sliced onion or cucumber.

COOK'S TIPS
The flavor of the dish will improve if it is left overnight. If you intend to do this, reduce the cooking time by 10 minutes and insure the meat is thoroughly heated before serving the next day. If, at the end of the cooking the flavor is too hot for your taste, add a little more yogurt or sour cream.

FREEZING
Transfer to a rigid container, cool quickly, then seal, label and freeze up to 3 months. To serve: Thaw in refrigerator overnight, then reheat until the chicken is heated through and the sauce is bubbling. Stir in a little chicken broth or water if the sauce is too thick. Continue from the beginning of stage 4.

● 460 calories per portion

Rosé chicken

SERVES 4

3-3½ lb broiler/fryer
salt and freshly ground black pepper
2 tablespoons butter or margarine
2 sprigs fresh tarragon, chopped, or 1 teaspoon dried tarragon
1 small onion, halved
⅔ cup rosé vermouth
2 good pinches paprika
2 teaspoons tomato paste
1 tablespoon cornstarch
¼ cup milk
⅔ cup chicken broth
1-2 teaspoons lemon juice, according to taste

1 Preheat the oven to 375°.
2 Pat the chicken dry with paper towels, then sprinkle inside and out with salt and pepper.
3 Place half the butter inside the chicken with half the tarragon and the onion halves. Truss with thread or fine string.
4 Place the chicken in an ovenproof dish [!] and spread with the remaining butter. Sprinkle over the remaining tarragon, then pour the vermouth around the chicken.
5 Roast in the oven 1¼ hours or until the chicken is tender and the juices run clear when the thickest part of the thigh is pierced with a skewer. Baste occasionally during the cooking time.
6 Remove the chicken from the dish and discard the trussing thread. Place the chicken on a warmed serving platter and keep hot in the lowest possible oven.
7 To make the sauce: Pour the juices from the chicken into a saucepan. Stir in a pinch of paprika and the tomato paste. In a bowl, blend the cornstarch to a paste with the milk, gradually stir in the chicken broth and add to the pan. Stir well to combine, bring to a boil, then simmer 2 minutes, stirring constantly. Taste and adjust seasoning, then add lemon juice to taste, for a sharper flavor. [*]
8 Pour a little of the sauce over the chicken and sprinkle with the remaining paprika. Serve at once, with the remaining sauce passed separately.

TIME
Preparation 10 minutes and cooking time 1¼ hours. Last-minute finishing touches, 10 minutes.

WATCH POINT
Choose an ovenproof dish just large enough to take the chicken. The vermouth will evaporate too quickly if a large space is left around the bird.

FREEZING
Cut the chicken into portions, arrange in a freezer container and cover completely with the sauce. Cool quickly, then seal, label and freeze up to 6 months. To serve: reheat from frozen in a 400° oven about 1 hour, or until thawed.

PRESSURE COOKING
Weigh the chicken and calculate exact cooking time at 7 minutes per 1 lb. Pre-brown the chicken, drain, then stand on the trivet, rimside down. Pour vermouth and 1¼ cups broth into base of cooker. Bring to high (H) pressure, then cook for calculated time. Release pressure quickly. Make the sauce using liquid in base of cooker.

● 395 calories per portion

Crunchy chicken salad

SERVES 4

1¾ cups boneless cooked chicken
1 cup brown rice
2½ cups chicken broth
1 large red pepper, seeded and finely chopped
1 bunch scallions, chopped
¼ lb frozen peas, cooked and cooled
½ cup grated carrot
¾ cup walnuts, roughly chopped
¾ cup mayonnaise
1 tablespoon tomato paste
generous pinch of sugar
1 tablespoon chopped parsley (optional)

DRESSING

2 tablespoons olive or salad oil
1 tablespoon lemon juice
2 teaspoons wine vinegar or dry white wine
pinch of dry mustard
salt and freshly ground black pepper

1 Cook the brown rice in the chicken broth about 45 minutes until tender. If necessary, top up the pan with boiling water during the latter part of the cooking time.
2 Meanwhile, make the dressing: Combine all the ingredients in a screw-top jar and shake well to mix.
3 Drain any excess liquid from the rice, then mix in the red pepper, scallions, peas and carrot.
4 While the rice is still warm, fork the dressing through the mixture. Cover the bowl with plastic wrap and chill in the refrigerator at least 1 hour.
5 When ready to serve, add the walnuts to the rice and mix thoroughly. Spoon into a serving dish and arrange the cooked chicken on top of the rice.
6 Mix the mayonnaise with the tomato paste and sugar. It should be the consistency of a coating sauce; if it is too thick, stir in a little hot water.
7 Carefully spoon the mayonnaise on top of the cooked chicken, then sprinkle the top with chopped parsley, if liked.

Cook's Notes

TIME
The rice will take 45 minutes to cook and 1 hour to chill, during which time the other preparations can be completed.

COOK'S TIP
Brown rice takes longer to cook than long-grain white rice, but has a lovely, nutty flavor. It will absorb the dressing better if you fork it through while the rice is still quite warm.

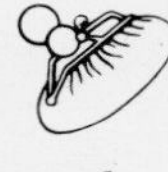

ECONOMY
Cut down the cooking time for the rice by soaking it for 2 hours in cold water before cooking.

VARIATIONS
Add finely chopped celery, green peppers, drained canned whole kernel corn, chopped green beans or any other suitable crisp vegetable to the salad.

● 865 calories per portion

Chicken paprikash

SERVES 4
4 chicken pieces, skinned
1 tablespoon butter or margarine
1 lb onions, finely chopped
1 clove garlic, crushed (optional)
1 tablespoon paprika
salt and freshly ground black pepper
about ⅔ cup hot chicken broth
½ cup dairy sour cream
chopped chives, to garnish

1 Preheat the oven to 350°.
2 Melt the butter in a large, shallow flameproof casserole big enough to take the chicken pieces in a single layer (see Cook's tip). Add onions and garlic, if using, cover and cook gently abut 45 minutes until a soft, golden brown purée is formed.
3 Raise the heat slightly, then sprinkle in the paprika and salt and pepper to taste. Add the chicken and spoon over the onion mixture.
4 Cover the casserole and bake in the oven 45 minutes or until the juices run clear when the thickest part of the chicken flesh is pierced with a skewer. Check the casserole contents regularly and add a little broth from time to time if the chicken appears to be becoming a little too dry.
5 Heat the sour cream in a pan; do not boil, or it will curdle. Pour over the chicken; sprinkle with chives and serve at once.

Cook's Notes

TIME
Preparation 10 minutes, total cooking time about 1½ hours.

COOK'S TIP
If you do not have a casserole big enough to take the chicken in 1 layer use a large, lidded skillet and cook the complete dish on the top of the range.

WATCHPOINT
Be careful that the purée does not become too liquid – it should be thick enough to coat the chicken without forming a sauce.

SERVING IDEAS
Serve with savory rice made by adding some cooked chopped mushrooms and cooked chopped green pepper and onion to plain boiled rice.

FREEZING
Cool quickly, then freeze in a rigid container up to 2 months. To serve: Thaw overnight in the refrigerator, pour in ⅔ cup hot chicken broth, reheat in oven at 375° 40 minutes or until bubbling. Continue from stage 5.

● 290 calories per portion

Chicken lasagne

SERVES 4

6 strips lasagne (see Buying guide)
salt
1 teaspoon vegetable oil
freshly ground black pepper
1 cup grated Cheddar cheese
butter, for greasing

CHICKEN SAUCE

3 tablespoons vegetable oil
1 large onion, sliced
¼ lb streaky bacon, chopped
4 tablespoons all-purpose flour
1¼ cups chicken broth
1 can (about 8 oz) tomatoes
1⅔ cups boneless cooked chicken, chopped (see Buying guide)
1 tablespoon tomato paste

WHITE SAUCE

2 tablespoons butter or margarine
4 tablespoons all purpose flour
pinch of freshly ground nutmeg
1¼ cups milk

1 Preheat the oven to 350° and then thoroughly grease a shallow ovenproof dish. ✳

2 Make the chicken sauce: Heat the oil in a skillet, add the onion and cook gently until soft and lightly colored. Add the bacon and cook 1 minute.

3 Sprinkle in the flour and cook 1 minute, stirring, until straw-colored. Remove from the heat and gradually stir in broth, tomatoes, chicken and tomato paste.

4 Return to the heat and bring to a boil, stirring constantly, then lower the heat and simmer 3 minutes. Remove from the heat and set aside.

5 Bring a large pan of salted water to a boil and cook the lasagne with the oil 10 minutes.

6 Meanwhile, make the white sauce: Melt the butter in a saucepan, sprinkle in the flour and nutmeg and stir over low heat 2 minutes until straw-colored. Remove from the heat and gradually stir in the milk, return to the heat again and simmer, stirring, until thick and smooth. Set aside.

7 Drain the lasagne and pat dry with paper towels.

8 Spread half the chicken sauce in the bottom of the greased ovenproof dish and sprinkle with salt and pepper. Place 3 strips of lasagne on top.

9 Spread the remaining chicken sauce over the lasagne, sprinkle with more salt and pepper and cover with a second layer of lasagne. Pour the white sauce over the lasagne and sprinkle with salt and pepper.

10 Sprinkle the grated cheese over the top of the white sauce, then bake in the oven 1 hour until bubbling and golden. If the topping is not golden at the end of the cooking time, preheat the broiler to high and transfer the lasagne to the broiler 2-3 minutes to brown the cheese. Serve hot, straight from the dish.

Cook's Notes

TIME

Preparation 35 minutes, cooking 1 hour.

BUYING GUIDE

Lasagne varies in width, from one manufacturer to another – "strips" of lasagne are narrow; "sheets" are wider.

For 1⅔ cups boneless chicken, buy 2 large chicken breasts and cook, skin and bone them before using, or buy half a roasted chicken and simply remove the meat.

FREEZING

Do not pre-cook the lasagne strips. Arrange them over the chicken sauce in layers as in stage 8. Cook the lasagne in a foil freezer container, cool quickly, then seal, label and freeze. Store up to 1 month. To serve: Reheat from frozen, uncovered, in the foil container in a 400° oven 1½ hours until bubbling.

• 655 calories per portion

Chicken polka pie

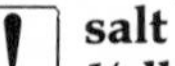

SERVES 4

2 cups boneless cooked chicken, cut into bite-sized pieces (see Buying guide)
2 lb potatoes
salt
¼ lb frozen mixed vegetables with whole kernel corn
1¼ cups package parsley sauce mix
1¼ cups milk
1 teaspoon Worcestershire sauce
pinch of freshly ground nutmeg
freshly ground black pepper
3 hard-boiled eggs, chopped (see Freezing)
3 tablespoons butter or margarine
¾ cup grated Cheddar cheese
¼ cup flaked almonds (optional)

1 Cook the potatoes in boiling salted water about 15 minutes until tender but still firm. At the same time, cook the frozen vegetables according to package directions.

2 While the potatoes and vegetables are cooking, make up the parsley sauce with the milk according to package directions. Stir in the Worcestershire sauce, nutmeg and salt and pepper to taste.

3 Drain the frozen vegetables and fold into the sauce with the chicken and hard-boiled eggs. Simmer over very gentle heat until the chicken is thoroughly heated through, stirring occasionally.

4 Meanwhile, drain the potatoes and, when cool enough to handle, slice thickly. Grease a shallow flameproof dish [*] with 1 tablespoon butter. Preheat the broiler to high.

5 Pour the chicken mixture into the dish and level the surface. Place the potato slices on top, overlapping them so they cover the chicken mixture completely. Dot with the remaining butter and sprinkle with the cheese.

6 Place under the heated broiler 7-10 minutes until crisp and golden brown. Sprinkle the flaked almonds over the top, if using, and replace under the broiler until the almonds are lightly toasted. [!] Serve at once, straight from the dish.

Cook's Notes

TIME
Preparation and cooking about 1 hour; broiling 7-10 minutes.

FREEZING
If freezing this dish, leave out the hard-boiled eggs because they become rubbery in the freezer. Make the pie up to the end of stage 6 in a freezerproof casserole dish instead of the flameproof dish. Leave until cold, then seal, label and freeze up to 6 months. To serve: Cook from frozen, uncovered, in a 400° oven about 1 hour or until heated through and golden brown.

SERVING IDEAS
As the dish already contains potatoes and vegetables, serve with a contrasting, crisp salad of lettuce and watercress. Sliced tomatoes can be used as a garnish in place of the almonds.

VARIATION
Use cheese or onion sauce mix instead of parsley.

COOK'S TIP
For an even quicker dish to prepare use canned new potatoes for the topping. Drain them well.

WATCHPOINT
Keep a strict eye on the dish at this stage, the almonds can easily burn and spoil the flavor.

BUYING GUIDE
Left-over cooked chicken can be used for this dish, but if you are buying ready-cooked chicken pieces, you will need 3 with a total weight of about 1¼ lb in order to have 2 cups meat when all the skin and bones have been removed.

• 620 calories per portion

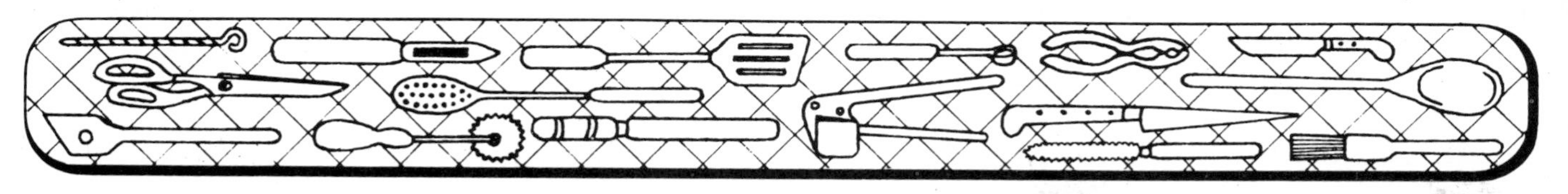

Turkey parcels

SERVES 4
8 turkey scallops (see Buying guide)
1 cup dried apricots, soaked overnight and drained
⅓ cup ground almonds
¼ cup butter or margarine
½ cup dry white wine
salt and freshly ground black pepper
watercress, to garnish
butter, for greasing

1 Preheat the oven to 375°. Cut 8 pieces of foil, large enough to enclose the turkey scallops, and then lightly grease them with butter.
2 Roughly chop two-thirds of the apricots and mix in a bowl with the ground almonds. Spread equal portions of this mixture on one half of each scallop and then fold the other half over to make a sandwich.
3 Place each stuffed scallop on a piece of greased foil. Fold up the sides of the foil without sealing, put a knob of butter on each scallop and then pour 1 tablespoon wine over each. Season well with salt and pepper and loosely fold the foil to enclose the stuffed scallop. Seal and place the parcels on a cookie sheet and cook in the oven about 30 minutes.
4 To serve the scallops: Remove the foil and transfer the meat to a warmed serving platter, pour over the juices, then garnish with the remaining apricot halves and top with the watercress.

Cook's Notes

TIME
Allow 30 minutes for preparation and 30 minutes for cooking.

SERVING IDEAS
Serve with croquette potatoes, green beans or a crisp fennel and zucchini salad.

VARIATIONS
Use pork scallops or chicken breasts instead of the turkey. Replace the dried apricots with ½ cup of thick apple sauce flavored with ground nutmeg, or use 1½ tablespoons of plain yogurt in each parcel instead of the butter and wine.

BUYING GUIDE
Turkey scallops, thin slices of meat cut from the breasts, are available in packages at large supermarkets. You will need 2 scallop parcels per person.

● 420 calories per portion

Creamy almond turkey

SERVES 4

1 lb turkey fillets/scallops
2 tablespoons butter
2 teaspoons all-purpose flour
1¼ cups chicken broth
2 teaspoons tomato paste
2 tablespoons ground almonds
salt and freshly ground black pepper
¼ cup flaked almonds
⅓ cup light cream

1 Preheat the oven to 350°.
2 Melt the butter in a shallow flameproof casserole. Add the turkey fillets and cook over moderate heat 2-3 minutes on each side until lightly colored. Remove from the casserole with a slotted spoon and reserve.
3 Sprinkle the flour into the hot butter in the casserole and stir over low heat 1-2 minutes until straw-colored. Gradually stir in the chicken broth, then simmer, stirring, until thick and smooth.
4 Stir in the tomato paste and ground almonds and mix well. Season to taste with salt and pepper. Return the turkey fillets to the casserole. Cover and bake in the oven 30 minutes.
5 Meanwhile, brown the flaked almonds: Put them into a heated, ungreased, skillet and shake the pan over the heat until the almonds are light brown all over. [!]
6 Add the cream to the cooked turkey and stir it into the sauce. Sprinkle over the browned almonds and serve at once.

Cook's Notes

TIME
Preparation takes 20 minutes. Cooking in the oven takes about 30 minutes.

VARIATION
Chicken breast may be used instead of turkey.

WATCHPOINT
Watch the almonds carefully as they can burn.

SERVING IDEAS
For a pretty color contrast with the pink sauce, serve with green pasta and spinach or broccoli.

• 285 calories per portion

Macaroni turkey

SERVES 4

1½ lb boneless turkey meat, cut into 1-inch cubes (see Buying guide)
1 tablespoon vegetable oil
¼ cup butter or margarine
1 large onion, chopped
2 celery stalks, chopped
2 teaspoons all-purpose flour
1 can (about 10 oz) condensed cream of chicken soup
1¼ cups chicken broth
salt and freshly ground black pepper
2 teaspoons Dijon-style mustard
1⅓ cups whole wheat macaroni
½ lb mushrooms, sliced
2 tablespoons chopped parsley
½ cup fresh white bread crumbs
tomato slices, to garnish

1 Heat oil and half the butter in a large skillet. Add the onion and celery and cook gently 1-2 minutes. Add the turkey and cook briskly a further 3-4 minutes, stirring often, to brown on all sides.

2 Sprinkle the flour into the skillet and stir over low heat 1-2 minutes. Remove from the heat and stir in the soup and the chicken broth. Return to heat and bring to a boil, stirring. Season to taste. Lower the heat, add the mustard and simmer for about 20 minutes.

3 Preheat the oven to 400°.

4 Meanwhile, bring a large pan of salted water to a boil and cook the macaroni for 10 minutes. Drain well. Melt the remaining butter in the rinsed-out pan, add the macaroni and stir it well to coat thoroughly.

5 Spoon the macaroni over the base of a large ovenproof dish.

6 Stir the sliced mushrooms into the turkey mixture and spoon over macaroni. Sprinkle with the parsley and bread crumbs and bake 20 minutes. Serve hot, straight from the dish, garnished with tomato slices.

Cook's Notes

TIME
Preparation takes about 20 minutes, cooking time about 40 minutes.

BUYING GUIDE
Boneless light and dark turkey meat, cut into chunks, is available in casserole packs from the refrigerator and freezer cabinets of large supermarkets and freezer centers. Thaw frozen turkey meat before using in this recipe.

● 600 calories per portion

Turkey in breadcrumbs

SERVES 4

4 turkey fillets/scallops, each weighing about ¼ lb, thoroughly thawed if frozen
2 tablespoons all-purpose flour
salt and freshly ground black pepper
⅓ cup fresh white bread crumbs
2 eggs
vegetable oil, for cooking
tomato wedges and parsley sprigs, to garnish

SAUCE

1 tablespoon butter
2 tomatoes peeled and chopped
½ lb frozen whole kernel corn (see Cook's tip)
2 tablespoons heavy cream

1 Place the turkey fillets between 2 large sheets of waxed paper and beat with a rolling pin or mallet until they are very thin and twice their original size.

2 Preheat the oven to 225°.

3 Spread the flour out on a flat plate and season with salt and pepper. Spread the bread crumbs out on a separate flat plate. Beat the eggs in a shallow dish.

4 Dip the turkey scallops into the flour, then into beaten egg, and then into bread crumbs, to coat evenly.

5 Pour oil into a large skillet to a depth of about ¼ inch. Heat the oil, add 2 turkey scallops and cook over brisk heat about 3 minutes on each side, until golden brown and crisp.

6 Drain the scallops on both sides on paper towels. Transfer to a warmed serving dish and keep warm in the oven while cooking the remaining scallops in same way.

7 While the last 2 scallops are cooking, make the sauce: Melt the butter in a small saucepan, add the tomatoes and cook 1-2 minutes until very soft. Stir in the corn and cook 3 minutes, then stir in the cream and heat through gently. Season with salt and pepper.

8 Drain the last 2 turkey scallops on both sides on paper towels and transfer to the serving dish. Garnish with tomato wedges and parsley sprigs and serve at once, with the sauce passed separately in a warmed gravyboat.

Cook's Notes

TIME
Preparation takes about 25 minutes. Cooking, including making the sauce, takes 15 minutes.

SERVING IDEAS
Serve with sautéed potatoes and peas cooked in the French way with tiny onions, shredded lettuce and diced bacon.

COOK'S TIP
The corn does not need to be thawed: Just stir into the pan and heat thoroughly without overcooking, as this will toughen it.

● 435 calories per portion

Farmhouse turkey and ham pie

SERVES 4

1 package (17 oz) frozen puff pastry, thawed
2 cups cooked turkey, chopped
1½ cups cooked ham, chopped
2 hard-boiled eggs, quartered
a little beaten egg, to glaze

SAUCE

2 tablespoons butter or margarine
4 tablespoons flour
1¼ cups milk
finely grated rind and juice of ½ lemon
1 tablespoon chopped fresh parsley
salt and freshly ground black pepper

1 Preheat the oven to 425°.

2 Roll out the pastry on a lightly floured surface to a shape slightly larger than the circumference of a deep pie dish. Cut off a long narrow strip all around edge. Reserve with other trimmings.

3 Mix the turkey and ham together in the pie dish and arrange the quartered eggs ✳ on top.

4 Make the sauce: Melt the butter in a small saucepan, sprinkle in the flour and stir over low heat 1-2 minutes until straw-colored. Remove from the heat and gradually stir in the milk. Return to the heat and simmer, stirring, until it is thick and smooth.

5 Remove from the heat and stir in the lemon rind and juice, and the parsley. Season to taste with salt and pepper and allow to cool. Pour evenly over the turkey and ham in the pie dish.

6 Brush the rim of the pie dish with water, and then press the narrow strip of pastry all around the rim. Brush the strip with a little more water, then place the large piece of pastry on top. Trim the edge of the pastry, then knock up the flute.

7 Make leaves with the pastry trimmings, brush the undersides with water and place on top of the pie. Brush with beaten egg and make a small hole in the center of the pastry top.

8 Bake in the oven 25-30 minutes until the pastry is well risen and golden brown. Serve hot or cold.

Cook's Notes

TIME
Preparation takes about 20 minutes, baking in the oven 25-30 minutes.

SPECIAL OCCASION
Add 1 tablespoon dry white wine instead of the lemon juice to the sauce.

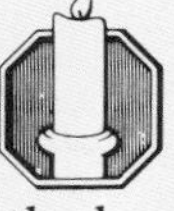

FREEZING
Omit the hard-boiled eggs in stage 3, then prepare the pie to stage 7, but do not brush with beaten egg. Open freeze until solid, then wrap in a freezer bag. Seal, label and return to the freezer up to 2 months. To serve: Remove from bag, thaw overnight in the refrigerator, then brush with beaten egg and make a hole in the top. Bake in a 425° oven for about 30 minutes.

SERVING IDEAS
A green salad is the best accompaniment to the turkey and ham pie.

• 825 calories per portion

Stuffed turkey drumsticks

SERVES 4

4 turkey drumsticks, unskinned
¼ lb streaky bacon slices, chopped
1 onion, finely chopped
1 red pepper, seeded and finely chopped
½ cup button mushrooms, finely chopped
½ cup fresh white bread crumbs
3 tablespoons finely chopped fresh parsley
1 egg, beaten
salt and freshly ground black pepper
vegetable oil, for brushing

1 Preheat oven to 350°.
2 Bone the drumsticks: With a sharp knife cut through the tendons at each end of the bone, then starting at the thigh end work the flesh down towards the knuckle and ease the flesh over the narrow end, to expose the bone.
3 Place the blade of the knife across the bone at the knuckle. Bang the knife sharply with a rolling pin to cut through the bone, so that only a small piece is left inside the flesh. [!]
4 Put the bacon in a skillet and cook over gentle heat until the fat runs (see Cook's tips). Add the onion and red pepper and cook gently 5 minutes until softened. Stir in the mushrooms and cook 2 minutes.
5 Put the cooked bacon and vegetables in a bowl and combine with the bread crumbs, parsley and egg, stirring well to mix. Season with salt and pepper.
6 Allow the stuffing mixture to cool, then pack it into the drumsticks. Secure the ends with wooden toothpicks and place drumsticks in a small roasting pan. Brush with oil and sprinkle with salt (see Cook's tips).
7 Bake in the oven 45-50 minutes, until golden. Remove the toothpicks and serve hot or cold.

Cook's Notes

TIME
Preparation, including boning the drumsticks, making the stuffing and stuffing the drumsticks takes about 1 hour. Cooking in the oven takes about 50 minutes.

FREEZING
Cool quickly, open freeze until solid, then pack in a freezer bag. Seal, label and return to the freezer up to 6 months. To serve: Thaw at room temperature 3-4 hours, then serve cold (the drumsticks tend to go dry if reheated after freezing.

WATCHPOINT
During the boning process be careful not to split the skin.

COOK'S TIPS
The bacon cooks in its own fat: No extra fat or oil for cooking is needed.
Sprinkling with salt makes the skin deliciously crisp.

• 275 calories per portion

Roast duck with grapes

SERVES 4

1 duck, weighing 4½-5 lb, giblets reserved
salt
1 small onion, quartered
bouquet garni
freshly ground black pepper
2 cups water
grapes and watercress, to garnish

SAUCE

1 onion, very finely chopped
4 tablespoons all-purpose flour
1¼ cups duck giblet stock
⅔ cups dry white wine
¼ lb each green and black grapes, quartered and pitted
2 tablespoons heavy cream

1 Preheat the oven to 350°.
2 Pat the duck dry inside and out with paper towels. Prick the skin all over and sprinkle with salt.
3 Weigh the duck and calculate the roasting time at 30 minutes per 1 lb. Place the duck breast side up, on a broiler rack or trivet in a roasting pan. Roast, without basting, in the oven for the calculated cooking time, until the skin is brown and crisp, and the juices run clear when thigh is pierced with a fine skewer.
4 Meanwhile, rinse the giblets in cold water and place in a saucepan together with the quartered onion and bouquet garni. Season with salt and pepper and cover with the water. Bring to a boil, then lower heat and simmer gently 1 hour. Strain and set aside.
5 Drain the cooked duck well, saving 2 tablespoons drippings (see Economy). Place the duck on a warmed serving dish and keep hot in the oven turned down to 225°, while making sauce.
6 Pour the 2 tablespoons of hot duck drippings into a small saucepan. Add the chopped onion, cover the pan and cook gently 10 minutes, shaking the pan from time to time until the onion is soft and golden brown. Sprinkle in the flour and stir over low heat 1-2 minutes then gradually stir in 1¼ cups of the strained giblet stock and the wine. Bring to a boil, and simmer 2 minutes, stirring, until thickened.
7 Add the grapes and heat through gently a further 2 minutes. Remove from the heat and stir in the cream. Pour into a warmed bowl or gravy boat and pass separately with the roast duck (see Cook's tip), garnished with grapes and watercress.

Cook's Notes

TIME
Preparation takes about 25 minutes, cooking 2¼-2½ hours, including roasting the duck, preparing the stock and making the sauce.

SERVING
This makes a perfect Christmas dinner for 4 people and a more suitable alternative to turkey, which is best for serving larger numbers.

COOK'S TIP
For easier serving, cut the duck in half lengthwise, using sharp kitchen scissors to cut down the breastbone and along backbone. Then cut each half into 2 even portions.

Arrange the 4 portions on a warmed serving dish.

ECONOMY
Strain the remaining drippings from the duck into a bowl. Cover and keep in the refrigerator for roasting potatoes. Duck drippings can also be used for roasting parsnips.

• 490 calories per portion

Honey duck salad

SERVES 4

4½ lb duck, thawed if frozen
salt
2 tablespoons clear honey
1 tablespoon hot water

SALAD GARNISH

2 heads endive leaves, separated
1 bunch watercress, divided into small sprigs
2 oranges, divided into segments

DRESSING

4 tablespoons vegetable oil
1 tablespoon tarragon vinegar
1 tablespoon fresh orange juice
pinch of sugar
½ teaspoon Dijon-style mustard
salt and freshly ground black pepper

1 Preheat the oven to 350°.
2 Pat the duck dry inside and out with paper towels. Prick the skin all over with a fork and sprinkle evenly with salt.
3 Place the duck breast side up, on a rack in a roasting pan. Roast in the oven 1 hour, then drain off the fat from the pan. Blend the honey with the hot water and brush the duck all over with the mixture.
4 Return the honey duck to the oven and roast a further 1¼ hours, basting 2-3 times to glaze and brown. Drain the duck over the pan, transfer to a plate and leave until completely cold (3-4 hours).
5 Divide the duck into 4 (see Preparation). Arrange on a serving dish. Garnish with endive leaves, watercress sprigs and orange segments.
6 Place ingredients for dressing in a screw-top jar, with salt and pepper to taste, and shake well together. Sprinkle over the salad just before serving.

Cook's Notes

TIME
Roasting the honey duck takes about 2¼ hours. Allow 3-4 hours cooling time. Finishing the duck salad takes about 15 minutes.

SERVING IDEAS
Serve this tasty and refreshing salad with thinly sliced potatoes that have been fried until crisp. Or serve the duck with a colorful rice salad or pasta salad.

VARIATIONS
Garnish the serving dish with cold, lightly cooked green beans, carrot curls and cauliflower flowerets instead of the endive, watercress and orange salad.

PREPARATION
To divide the duck into 4 portions:

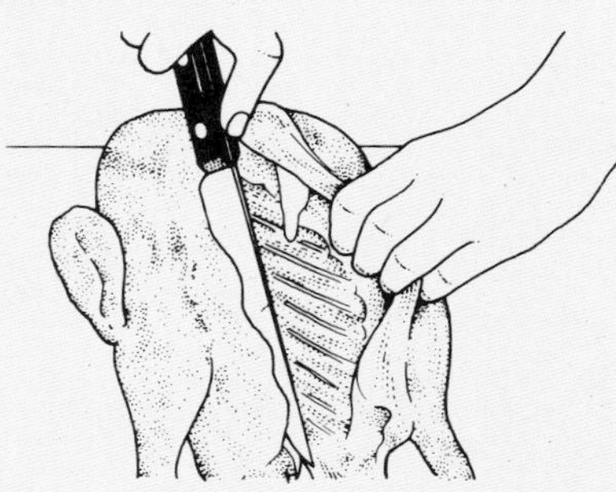

1 *Using a very sharp knife, cut the duck lengthwise down breastbone. Pry open, then cut lengthwise again, as close to the backbone as possible.*

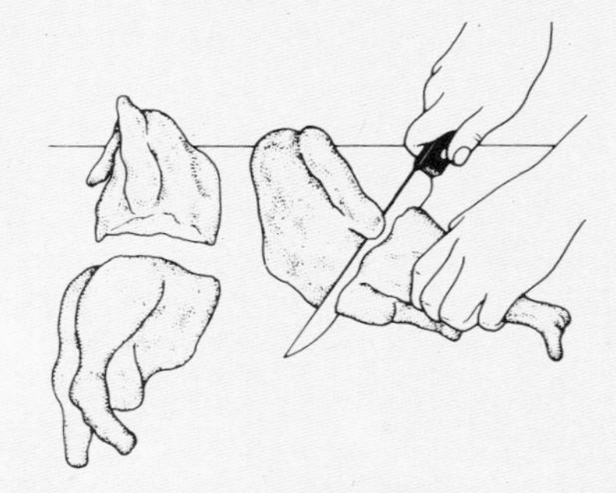

2 *Cut each duck half across into 2 pieces, inserting the knife between leg and wing.*

● 865 calories per portion

Duck 'n' beans

SERVES 4

- **4 duck pieces, each weighing about ¾ lb, thawed if frozen (see Buying guide)**
- **salt and freshly ground black pepper**
- **1 onion, chopped**
- **1 clove garlic, crushed (optional)**
- **2 cups chicken broth**
- **1 tablespoon medium sherry**
- **1 can (about 15 oz) baked beans in tomato sauce**
- **1 tablespoon tomato catsup**
- **⅓ lb spicy garlic sausage, chopped**
- **1 teaspoon dried thyme**
- **1 bay leaf**

TOPPING

- **4 tablespoons chopped fresh parsley**
- **1 cup fresh white bread crumbs**

1 Preheat the oven to 375°.

2 Prick the duck pieces all over with a fork, season with salt and pepper and place on a rack in a roasting pan. Roast 1¼ hours, until the duck pieces are cooked through (the juices run clear when the meat is pierced with a fine skewer). Remove the duck pieces from the pan, drain on paper towels and place in a large casserole. Turn the oven down to 350°.

3 Drain off all but 1 tablespoon fat from the pan and transfer the pan to the top of the stove. Add the onion and garlic, if using, and cook gently 2 minutes.

4 Gradually stir in the broth and sherry and bring to a boil, stirring constantly. Stir in the baked beans in their sauce, the tomato catsup, garlic sausage, thyme and bay leaf. Season to taste with salt and freshly ground black pepper.

5 Pour the mixture over the duck pieces in the casserole. Cover and cook the casserole in the oven 30 minutes.

6 Increase the oven heat to 425°. Mix the parsley and bread crumbs together and sprinkle evenly over the surface of the casserole. Return to the oven and cook a further 15 minutes, uncovered, to brown the topping. Serve hot.

Cook's Notes

TIME
Preparation takes about 20 minutes, cooking about 2¼ hours.

BUYING GUIDE
Duck pieces, consisting of the breast and wing, are available from high-quality butchers, large supermarkets and freezer centers.

SERVING IDEAS
Serve with jacket-baked potatoes and a salad

● 840 calories per portion

Spiced fried herrings

SERVES 4

8 herrings, each weighing about ¼ lb, heads removed, cleaned, boned and roes reserved (optional)
1 egg yolk
1 tablespoon milk
3 tablespoons all-purpose flour
½ teaspoon paprika
salt and freshly ground black pepper
vegetable oil, for cooking
lemon and lime wedges and coriander or parsley sprigs, to garnish

SPICE MIXTURE

3 tablespoons finely chopped fresh coriander or parsley
2 tablespoons olive or sunflower oil
1 tablespoon ground cumin
1 teaspoon paprika
½ teaspoon cayenne
½ teaspoon ground cinnamon
¼ teaspoon salt

1 Combine all ingredients for the spice mixture in a small bowl and mix well together. Open out the herrings and lay them flat, skin side down, on the board or work surface. Spread with spice mixture, then close the herrings up, cover and set aside in a cool place and leave for at least 3 hours.

2 Beat the egg yolk with the milk in a small bowl. Spread the flour out on a large flat plate and season with the paprika and salt and pepper to taste. Brush the herrings with the egg yolk mixture, then turn in the flour to coat evenly. Shake off the excess flour and reserve for the herring roes, if using.

3 Heat enough oil in a large skillet just to cover the base. Add 4 of the herrings and cook over moderate heat 4-5 minutes on each side until cooked through (the flesh should be opaque). Using a turner, transfer the cooked herrings to a warmed serving dish and keep warm. Heat a little more oil in the pan, add the remaining herrings and cook in the same way.

4 Turn the reserved roes, if using, in the remaining flour to coat evenly. Add to pan and cook 2-3 minutes, turning once, until just cooked. Remove and drain on paper towels.

5 Arrange the herrings with roes, if using, on serving dish. Garnish with lemon and lime wedges and coriander or parsley sprigs.

Cook's Notes

TIME
Preparation takes about 30 minutes. Allow 3 hours standing. Cooking then takes about 20-25 minutes.

SERVING
Serve with salad and rolls and butter.

• 410 calories per portion

Breton steaks

SERVES 4
½ lb cod or halibut steaks
salt and freshly ground black pepper
2 fl oz sweet vermouth

SAUCE
6 tablespoons butter
2 celery stalks, thinly sliced
2 small leeks, thinly sliced
1 small onion, thinly sliced
¼ lb mushrooms, thinly sliced
6 tablespoons all-purpose flour
⅔ cup milk

1 Preheat the oven to 350°.
2 Season the fish steaks well with salt and pepper. Arrange in the base of a casserole and pour over the vermouth. Cover and bake in the oven 30 minutes until the fish is tender and the flesh flakes easily when pierced with a knife.
3 Meanwhile, make the sauce: Melt half the butter in a large skillet, add the celery, leeks, onion and mushrooms and cook gently 5-6 minutes until soft. Set aside.
4 Using a turner, transfer the fish steaks to a warmed serving dish and keep warm in the oven turned to its lowest setting. Reserve the fish cooking juices.
5 In a small pan, melt remaining butter, sprinkle in the flour and stir over low heat 1-2 minutes until it is light straw-colored. Remove from the heat and gradually stir in the milk and the fish juices. Return to the heat and simmer, stirring, until thick and smooth.
6 Stir in the vegetables and heat through gently about 5 minutes. Pour the sauce over the fish steaks and serve the dish at once, while still piping hot (see Serving ideas).

Cook's Notes

TIME
This dish takes 1 hour to prepare and cook.

SERVING IDEAS
Serve with boiled new potatoes and broccoli or snow peas, and chilled white wine. Traditionally these fish steaks are garnished with small crescents of flaky pastry known as *fleurons*. To make *fleurons:* Cut out crescent shapes of puff pastry, using a metal cutter, and put them on a cookie sheet. At stage 4 remove fish steaks from the oven and keep warm. Increase heat to 400° and bake the *fleurons* 10 minutes.

DID YOU KNOW
In French cookery the term *à la bretonne*, when applied to fish, indicates that the dish is served with a sauce made with leeks, onions, celery and mushrooms.

● 405 calories per portion

Peanut flounder

SERVES 4

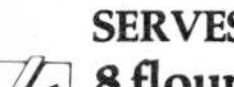

8 flounder fillets, each weighing about ¼ lb, skinned
1 large egg
2 tablespoons light cream
2 teaspoons lemon juice
salt and freshly ground black pepper
⅓ cup toasted bread crumbs (see Preparation)
3¼ cups peanuts, finely chopped (see Cook's tip)
1 tablespoon vegetable oil
2 tablespoons butter or margarine
lemon wedges, to serve

1 Put the egg, cream and lemon juice in a shallow bowl with salt and pepper to taste. Beat well to mix
2 Mix the bread crumbs and peanuts together on a plate.
3 Dip the fillets one by one into the egg mixture, lift by the tail to drain off the surplus egg, then coat in the bread crumb and peanut mixture. Press the crumbs into the fish and make sure each fillet is well coated on both sides.
4 Heat the oil and butter together in a large skillet until the mixture is foaming. Cook the fish, in 2 batches if necessary, 4-5 minutes on each side until they are all light golden in color. Then keep hot on paper towels until all are cooked, serve at once with wedges of lemon.

Cook's Notes

TIME
Preparation takes 20-25 minutes, cooking 10 minutes.

COOK'S TIP
Use ordinary raw peanuts, not the roasted or salted varieties, for this recipe. You can leave the skins on or remove them, before chopping, by rubbing them between your fingers. The peanuts can be chopped in a coffee grinder, blender or food processor, but do not chop too finely or the coating will not be crunchy.

PREPARATION
To make ¾ cup toasted bread crumbs, toast 4 thin slices of bread until golden on each side. Cut off the crusts, then work for a few seconds in a blender or food processor until reduced to crumbs.

● 430 calories per portion

Halibut special

SERVES 4
4 × ⅓ lb halibut steaks, skinned (see Buying guide)
⅔ cup white wine
1 tablespoon cornstarch
1 tablespoon cold water
fresh thyme, to garnish

TOPPING
2 tablespoons butter
1 onion, chopped
2 celery stalks, chopped
3 tomatoes peeled and chopped
¼ lb mushrooms, chopped
1 teaspoon chopped fresh thyme or ½ teaspoon dried thyme
salt and freshly ground black pepper

1 Preheat the oven to 325°.
2 Make the topping: Melt the butter in a saucepan. Add the onion and cook gently 5 minutes until soft and lightly colored. Add celery, tomatoes and mushrooms and cook 1 more minute, stirring once or twice. Add the thyme, season well with salt and pepper and set aside.
3 Arrange the halibut steaks in a single layer in a large shallow ovenproof dish. Spoon the vegetable mixture evenly over the halibut and pour around the white wine. Cover the dish with foil and bake in the oven about 40 minutes, until the halibut is cooked through and flakes easily when pierced with a sharp knife. Transfer the halibut steaks to a warmed serving dish.
4 Pour the cooking liquid into a small saucepan. Blend the cornstarch with the water to make a smooth paste and stir into the liquid. Bring to a boil, stirring constantly. Taste and adjust the seasoning if necessary, then pour over the halibut. Garnish with thyme and serve the halibut at once (see Serving ideas).

Cook's Notes

TIME
Preparation takes about 15 minutes, cooking in the oven about 40 minutes.

SERVING IDEAS
Serve simply with minted garden peas and potatoes gratin dauphinois (sliced and baked with cheese).

BUYING GUIDE
Halibut has a delicious delicate flavor, but is a more expensive white fish than cod or tilefish, which can be used instead. Some freezer centers sell economy packs of halibut.

● 230 calories per portion

Celery-stuffed trout

SERVES 4

4 rainbow trout, each weighing 10-12 oz, cleaned with heads and tails left on
butter, for greasing
celery leaves, to garnish

CELERY STUFFING

2 tablespoons butter or margarine
1 tablespoon vegetable oil
1 small onion, finely chopped
2 large celery stalks, finely chopped
⅔ cup fresh whole wheat bread crumbs
finely grated rind of 1 orange
finely grated rind of ½ lemon
1 teaspoon dried basil
1 teaspoon mustard powder
1 egg, beaten
2-3 tablespoons fresh orange juice
salt and freshly ground black pepper

1 Preheat the oven to 375°. Cut out and grease 4 foil squares each large enough to contain a whole rainbow trout.

2 Make celery stuffing: Heat the butter and oil in a saucepan, add the onion and cook gently 5 minutes until soft and lightly colored. Add celery and cook a further 2-3 minutes, stirring the mixture once or twice.

3 Remove from the heat and stir in the bread crumbs, orange and lemon rinds, the basil and mustard. Stir in the egg and enough orange juice just to bind. Season to taste with salt and pepper.

4 Spoon the stuffing into the trout cavities, dividing it equally between them. Place each trout on a piece of greased foil and seal tightly to make neat parcels (see Cook's tips).

5 Place the parcels on a cookie sheet and cook in the oven 25-30 minutes (see Cook's tips) until the fish is cooked through and the flesh flakes very easily when pierced with a sharp knife.

6 Open up the foil parcels and carefully transfer the trout to a warmed serving plate. Garnish with celery leaves and serve at once.

Cook's Notes

TIME

Preparation, including making the stuffing, takes 35 minutes. Cooking the trout in the oven takes about 25-30 minutes.

SERVING IDEAS

Top the fish with pats of herb butter if liked or garnish with thin orange and lemon slices or a sprinkling of herbs. Serve with potatoes boiled in their skins and oven-baked tomatoes.

COOK'S TIPS

The trout may be prepared in advance up to the end of stage 4, then refrigerated up to 4 hours until ready to cook.

To brown the fish: Turn back the foil for last 10 minutes.

VARIATION

Use fennel instead of celery and use the feathery leaves as a garnish.

● 505 calories per portion

Family fish pie

SERVES 4
1 lb cod or tilefish fillets
2 cups milk
1 small onion, quartered
2 bay leaves
4 cloves
6 whole black peppercorns
2 lb potatoes
salt
½ lb package frozen mixed vegetables
5 tablespoons butter or margarine
5 tablespoons milk
4 tablespoons chopped chives or finely chopped scallion tops
2 hard-boiled eggs, chopped
2 tablespoon chopped parsley
freshly ground black pepper
6 tablespoons all-purpose flour
1 tablespoon tomato paste
3 tomatoes, sliced to finish

1 Preheat the oven to 350°.
2 Put the fish in an ovenproof dish and cover with the milk. Add the onion quarters, bay leaves, cloves and peppercorns. Cover with foil or parchment paper and bake in the oven about 20 minutes until the fish flakes easily.
3 Meanwhile, cook the potatoes in boiling salted water 20 minutes until tender. Cook the frozen vegetables as directed on the package then drain.
4 When the fish is cooked, remove it from the dish and strain the cooking liquid into a cup or bowl. Increase the oven heat to 375°.
5 Drain the potatoes and mash with 2 tablespoons butter and the milk. Beat in the chives.
6 Flake the fish into a bowl, removing any skin and bones. Stir in the mixed vegetables, the hard-boiled eggs and the parsley. Season well with salt and pepper. Put the mixture in a large saucepan.
7 Melt the remaining 3 tablespoons butter gently in a separate saucepan and sprinkle in the flour. Stir over low heat 2 minutes until straw-colored, then remove from the heat and gradually stir in the reserved cooking liquid from the fish. Return to the heat, stir in the tomato paste and simmer, stirring constantly until the sauce is thick and smooth.
8 Pour the sauce into the fish mixture and fold gently to mix over low heat until heated through. Taste and adjust seasoning.
9 Turn the fish mixture into a buttered ovenproof dish. Spoon the mashed potato evenly over the top, level the surface and mark with a fork in a criss-cross pattern. ✱
10 Bake the fish in the oven 20-30 minutes until heated through. Arrange the sliced tomatoes on the top, then place the pie under a heated broiler 5 minutes, to brown the topping. Serve very hot, straight from the dish.

Cook's Notes

TIME
Preparing and cooking the fish and potatoes takes about 1 hour. Heating through the finished pie takes 20-30 minutes.

COOK'S TIP
This pie is a meal in itself, and is well worth the time it takes to prepare because you do not need to serve an accompanying vegetable with it.

ECONOMY
Any economical white fish may be used instead of cod.

SPECIAL OCCASION
Substitute a few frozen or canned shrimp, or canned mussels, for the mixed vegetables and mash the potatoes with light cream.

FREEZING
Make the pie without hard-boiled eggs and freeze after stage 9. Freeze up to 2 months. To serve: Thaw the pie overnight in the refrigerator then top with the tomatoes and give the pie slightly longer in the oven to heat through completely.

● 635 calories per portion

Salmon parcels

SERVES 4

4 × ½ lb salmon steaks, skinned and bones removed, thawed if frozen (see Buying guide)
3 tablespoons butter, softened
1 tablespoon finely chopped fresh parsley
½ teaspoon chopped fresh thyme, or ¼ teaspoon dried thyme
pinch of paprika
salt and freshly ground black pepper
2 sheets (17 oz package) frozen puff pastry, thawed
4 teaspoons lemon juice
little beaten egg, to glaze
4 lemon slices sprinkled with paprika, to garnish

1 Preheat the oven to 400°.

2 Put the butter in a small bowl with parsley, thyme and paprika. Season well with salt and pepper and beat with a wooden spoon until the herbs and spices are thoroughly blended with the butter.

3 Divide the pastry into 4 equal pieces. Roll each piece out on a lightly floured board into a circle about 8 inches in diameter, or large enough to enclose a salmon steak.

4 Spread each salmon steak with a quarter of prepared butter and place, buttered side up, on one-half of a pastry circle. Sprinkle the salmon steak with a little lemon juice and season lightly with salt and freshly ground black pepper.

5 Moisten edges of each pastry circle with water, then fold over to cover salmon and seal firmly to make neat parcels. [!] Make diagonal cuts on top and decorate with pastry trimming, if wished.

6 Dampen a cookie sheet and place the pastry parcels on it. Brush the parcels with beaten egg to glaze.

7 Bake just above center of the oven 20 minutes, then lower the heat to 350° and cook a further 15 minutes or until the pastry is well risen and golden brown. Serve the salmon parcels hot or cold, garnished with lemon slices dusted with paprika (see Serving ideas).

Cook's Notes

TIME
Preparation and cooking take about 1 hour.

BUYING GUIDE
Fresh salmon is at its best from May to July and many large supermarkets now sell trimmed steaks in their refrigerated cabinets. Frozen salmon steaks are available most of the year from large supermarkets and freezer centers.

WATCHPOINT
Do not try to make too tight a parcel or it may break open during baking. But be sure to seal parcels firmly.

SERVING IDEAS
Serve hot with new potatoes, garden peas and dairy sour cream dressing.

Serve cold with potato salad, sliced cucumber and lettuce salad and mayonnaise. Or, for picnics, wrap each parcel carefully in foil, then pack in a rigid container.

VARIATION
Omit the seasoned butter and spread each salmon steak with 1 teaspoon of dairy sour cream with chives before wrapping in pastry.

● 865 calories per portion

Tilefish thermidor

SERVES 6
1½ lb tilefish steaks
½ bay leaf
1 small carrot, sliced
½ small onion, sliced
4 black peppercorns (optional)
salt
½ cup butter or margarine
½ cup all-purpose flour
2½ cups milk
½ teaspoon dry mustard
pinch of cayenne
½ lb mushrooms, sliced
2 tablespoons dry sherry (optional)
⅓ cup grated Parmesan cheese
butter or margarine, for greasing
lemon slices, to garnish

1 Preheat the oven to 425°. Lightly grease an ovenproof baking dish.
2 Put the fish steaks in a wide shallow skillet in 1 layer, and scatter over the bay leaf, carrot, onion, peppercorns and salt. Add water to cover and bring to a boil. Lower the heat and cook gently until the fish flakes easily when tested with a fork, about 10 minutes. With a slotted spoon, or turner remove the fish carefully and keep warm.
3 Meanwhile, make the sauce: Melt ¼ cup butter in a small saucepan, sprinkle in the flour and stir over low heat 1-2 minutes until straw-colored. Remove from the heat and gradually stir in the milk. Return to the heat and simmer, stirring, until thick and smooth. Add the mustard powder, cayenne and salt to taste. Remove saucepan from the heat.
4 Melt the remaining butter in a skillet and cook the mushrooms about 3 minutes, stirring. Mix into the sauce with the sherry, if using.
5 Cut the fish into bite-sized pieces and carefully combine with the sauce. ✳
6 Pour the fish and sauce into the greased baking dish, sprinkle the Parmesan over the top and bake in the oven about 15 minutes until the top is golden brown and bubbling. Serve hot, straight from the dish, garnished with lemon.

Cook's Notes

TIME
Cooking the fish, preparing the sauce and cooking the mushrooms takes 20 minutes. Allow 15 minutes cooking time in the oven.

COOK'S TIP
This dish with its rich sauce may be prepared as much as 8 hours in advance, up to the end of stage 5. Allow to cool, cover with plastic wrap and refrigerate. Bring back to room temperature before baking.

VARIATIONS
Instead of Parmesan cheese, use grated Swiss or Emmental for a different flavor. Cod steaks may be substituted for tilefish.

SERVING IDEAS
Serve in vol-au-vent shells or with mashed potatoes. Broccoli or spinach are colorful accompaniments.

FREEZING
Cool the fish and mushroom sauce mixture quickly, pack into a foil container, seal, label and freeze up to 3 months. To serve: Thaw at room temperature and reheat in a 350° oven 30 minutes. Sprinkle over the cheese and bake as in stage 6. If you are serving the dish in frozen vol-au-vent shells, bake according to package directions.

● 335 calories per portion

Herby fish kabobs

SERVES 4

1½ lb boneless cod or tilefish steaks, skinned
2 tablespoons lemon juice
1 tablespoon vegetable oil
1 teaspoon Worcestershire sauce
1 tablespoon chopped mixed fresh herbs, or 1 teaspoon dried basil
good pinch of fresh chopped dill or dried chopped dillweed
salt and freshly ground black pepper
1 large green pepper, seeded
4 small tomatoes, halved
vegetable oil, for greasing

1 Cut the fish into 32 cubes and place on a large plate. In a bowl mix together the lemon juice, oil, Worcestershire sauce and herbs. Season well with salt and pepper and pour over the fish. Leave to stand for 5 minutes, turning the cubes of fish in the marinade from time to time.

2 Put the green pepper in a bowl and cover with boiling water. Leave to stand 5 minutes. Drain well, then cut into chunky pieces big enough to thread onto skewers.

3 Preheat the broiler to moderate. Slide alternative pieces of fish and green pepper onto 8 oiled skewers, 10 inches long. Complete each skewer with a halved tomato.

4 Place the skewers in a broiler pan and cook under the broiler 15-20 minutes, turning as necessary and basting with juices from the pan [!] until the fish is cooked through and lightly browned. Serve at once.

Cook's Notes

TIME
Preparation 15 minutes, cooking 15-20 minutes.

WATCHPOINT
The basting is necessary to avoid the fish becoming dry during cooking.

SERVING IDEAS
Prepare 4 portions of creamed potato and spread evenly over a shallow flameproof serving dish. Sprinkle with a little grated cheese and place under the hot broiler until golden brown. Keep hot below the broiler pan while cooking the fish. Arrange the fish kabobs on top of the browned potato and garnish with lemon slices and watercress. Serve with mayonnaise or tartar sauce.

In summer, cook the fish on skewers over the barbecue, and serve on a bed of shredded and chopped fresh salad ingredients.

VARIATIONS
Use raw cucumber instead of blanched green pepper. Add 1 tablespoon dry vermouth to the marinade.

● 180 calories per portion

Smoked fish and spinach roll

SERVES 4

1 lb smoked fish fillets
1¼ cups milk
2 bay leaves
1 lemon
½ lb frozen spinach
4 eggs, separated
3 hard-boiled eggs, finely chopped
¼ nutmeg, freshly ground
salt and freshly ground black pepper
3 tablespoons butter or margarine
2 tablespoons all-purpose flour
vegetable oil, for greasing

TO GARNISH
few tomato slices (optional)
parsley sprigs (optional)

1 Preheat the oven 350°.

2 Put the fish in an ovenproof dish and add the milk and bay leaves. Grate the rind from the lemon and reserve. Cut 2 slices from the lemon and put them on top of the fish. Cover the surface of the dish with aluminum foil and bake in the oven 15-20 minutes, until the flesh flakes easily.

3 Cook the spinach according to package directions, then drain thoroughly in a strainer pressing out all excess moisture with the back of a spoon.

4 Grease a 13½ × 9½ × 1 inch baking pan and line it with waxed paper. Grease the paper well (see Cook's tip).

5 Lift the fish from the pan with a slotted spoon and reserve the cooking liquid. Flake the flesh into a bowl, discarding all skin and bones. Mash the flesh well with a fork, then stir in the lemon rind.

6 Increase the oven temperature to 400°.

7 Beat the egg yolks and stir them into the fish. Beat the egg whites until stiff and standing in peaks, then fold into the fish. Turn the mixture out of the bowl into the jelly roll pan and spread it evenly over the base with a knife. Place in the oven and bake 10-12 minutes until the mixture is firm to the touch and beginning to brown.

8 Place the drained spinach in a saucepan with 1 tablespoon butter. Stir in the chopped egg, nutmeg and a little salt [!] and pepper to taste. Reserve, keeping warm.

9 Meanwhile, melt the remaining butter in a small saucepan, sprinkle in the flour and stir over low heat for 2 minutes until straw-colored. Remove from the heat and gradually strain in the reserved cooking liquid. Return to the heat and simmer, stirring, until thick and smooth. Keep warm.

10 Remove the fish from the oven and turn it out of the jelly roll pan onto a clean sheet of waxed paper. Gently ease the fish away from the lining paper. [!]

11 Spread the warm spinach mixture over the surface of the fish, then roll it up like a jelly roll, using the waxed paper to help you roll the fish. Slide the roll onto a warmed serving dish, join side down, and garnish the top with tomato slices and parsley sprigs, if liked. Cut a few slices off the roll and serve at once with the sauce passed separately.

Cook's Notes

TIME
This dish takes 1¼ hours to prepare and cook.

COOK'S TIP
To help avoid the fish mixture sticking to the aluminum foil during baking, brush the foil liberally with oil, or use a silicone paper or non-stick baking parchment, available from large supermarkets and hardware stores.

WATCHPOINTS
Add salt sparingly because the smoked fish has a salty flavor.

If the foil needs a little coaxing to come away from the fish mixture – run a knife carefully between them.

• 405 calories per portion

Squid salad

SERVES 4

1½ lb squid (see Buying guide)
7 tablespoons olive oil
1 clove garlic, crushed (optional)
2 scallions, finely chopped
3 tomatoes, peeled, seeded and chopped
1 small green and 1 small red pepper, seeded and roughly chopped
¼ lb shelled shrimp, thawed and drained if frozen
juice of ½ lemon
salt and freshly ground black pepper

1 Clean the squid and slice the flesh thinly into rings.

2 Heat 3 tablespoons of the oil in a skillet, add squid and garlic, if using, and cook, stirring often, about 10 minutes or until the squid is tender. Drain on paper towels and then set aside until the squid is completely cold.

3 Put the squid, scallions, tomatoes, peppers and shrimp into a serving dish. Blend the remaining oil with the lemon juice and season with salt and pepper. Pour the dressing over the squid salad, then, using two forks, gently toss until coated in dressing. Cover the salad and refrigerate 1 hour.

Cook's Notes

TIME
Total preparation takes about 45 minutes, including cleaning the squid. Allow 1 hour chilling time.

SERVING IDEAS
Serve with potato salad and a salad of lettuce and cucumber. Accompany with chunks of French bread and butter, and a glass of dry white wine.

BUYING GUIDE
Many fishstores now sell squid and it is becoming increasingly popular, as it represents good value for money. Small squid (no more than 4 inches long) are the most tender.

Ready-prepared, skinned and cleaned squid is sometimes sold, but it is more expensive.

● 375 calories per portion

Seafood macaroni bake

SERVES 4
¾ lb fresh or frozen cod or halibut fillets, skinned (see Cook's tips)
2½ cups milk
1 lemon (see Preparation)
1 bay leaf
3 whole black peppercorns
salt
¼ cup butter or margarine
½ lb mushrooms, thinly sliced
½ lb elbow macaroni, boiled, drained and rinsed (see Watchpoint)
1 jar (about 5 oz) mussels, drained
6 tablespoons all-purpose flour
½ lb shelled shrimp (see Cook's tips).
pinch of freshly grated nutmeg
freshly ground black pepper
butter, for greasing
extra lemon slices and unshelled fresh shrimp, to garnish

1 Put the fish in a large skillet with a lid and pour in enough of the milk to just cover. Add 2 slices of lemon, the bay leaf, peppercorns and a good pinch of salt. Bring gradually to a boil, then cover and turn off the heat under the pan. Leave to stand 5 minutes, then remove the fish with a turner. Flake the flesh into 1½-inch pieces, discarding any bones. Strain all the cooking liquid and reserve.
2 Melt 1½ tablespoons butter in the rinsed-out skillet, add the sliced mushrooms and cook 2-3 minutes. Stir in the lemon juice and remove from heat.
3 Preheat the oven to 350°.
4 Put the macaroni into a greased large ovenproof dish with the fish, mushrooms and mussels. Stir carefully to mix, without breaking up the fish.
5 Melt the remaining butter in a saucepan, sprinkle in the flour and stir over low heat 1-2 minutes until straw-colored. Remove from the heat and gradually stir in rest of milk and reserved cooking liquid. Return to the heat and simmer, stirring, until thick and smooth. Remove from heat, stir in the shrimp, nutmeg and salt and pepper to taste, then pour evenly over macaroni and fish mixture. Cook in the oven 20 minutes.
6 Garnish with lemon slices and unshelled shrimp, if liked, and serve hot, straight from the dish.

Cook's Notes

TIME
Preparation, 30 minutes; cooking in the oven, 20 minutes.

COOK'S TIPS
If using frozen fish there is no need to thaw before using: After bringing to a boil in stage 1, simmer for a few minutes until thoroughly thawed before turning off heat under pan.

If using frozen shrimp, there is no need to thaw them before adding to the sauce.

PREPARATION
Squeeze the juice from one-half of the lemon and slice the other half.

WATCHPOINT
Take care not to overcook the macaroni at this stage, as it will continue cooking in the oven. Rinsing it under cold running water after it has been boiled prevents it from sticking together.

● 610 calories per portion

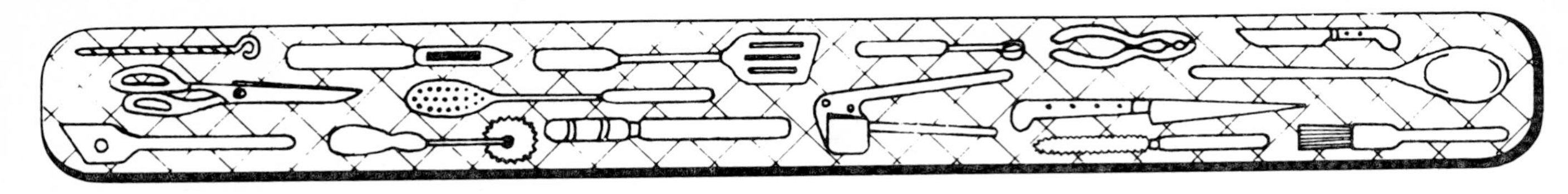

Mussel and shrimp pie

SERVES 4

1 sheet (½ of 17 oz package) frozen puff pastry, thawed
lightly beaten egg white, for glazing
lemon wedges, to garnish

FILLING

1 jar (about 1 lb) mussels in brine, drained
½ cup frozen shrimp, thawed
3 tablespoons butter or margarine
1 small onion, chopped
4 tablespoons all-purpose flour
1 cup less 2 tablespoons milk
⅓ cup dry white wine
salt and freshly ground black pepper
1 tablespoon chopped fresh parsley

1 On a lightly floured surface, roll out the pastry to 1½ inches larger all around than the top of an oven-proof pie dish. Invert the pie dish on the rolled out pastry and cut around the edge with a sharp knife to make a top. Then cut a strip the same width as the rim of the pie dish, from the outer edge.

2 Use the trimmings for decorations and refrigerate with the pastry.

3 Make the filling: Melt butter in a heavy-based saucepan, add the onion and cook gently about 5 minutes until it is soft and lightly colored. Sprinkle in the flour and stir over low heat 1-2 minutes. Remove from heat and gradually stir in milk. Return to heat and simmer, until thick.

4 Stir in the wine, mussels and shrimp and season to taste with salt and pepper. Simmer 2 minutes, then stir in the parsley. Pour the mixture into the pie dish and leave until cold (see Cook's tip).

5 Preheat the oven to 425°.

6 Dampen the rim of the dish with water. Place the pastry strip on the rim and press down lightly. Brush the strip with egg white, place pastry top on top of dish and press around the edge to seal. Trim any surplus pastry, then flute the edge. Brush pastry decorations with egg white and stick onto pastry top. Brush top with egg white.

7 Bake in the oven 20 minutes, then lower oven temperature to 375° and bake a further 15 minutes until the pastry is puffed up and golden. Serve the pie hot (see Serving ideas) with lemon wedges.

Cook's Notes

TIME
Preparation takes about 30 minutes and cooking 35 minutes. Allow extra time for cooling and chilling.

SERVING IDEAS
Serve pie with spinach and broiled tomatoes or with peas and whole kernel corn.

COOK'S TIP
The pie filling must be cold before covering or the pastry will be soggy.

• 430 calories per portion

Kedgeree special

SERVES 4-6

1 lb smoked fish fillets, thawed if frozen (see Did you know)
1¼ cups white or brown rice
2 tablespoons butter or margarine
1 onion, chopped
½ lb frozen mixed vegetables, thawed
½ cup plain yogurt
juice of ½ lemon
1 can (about 4 oz) smoked mussels, drained
¼ lb shelled shrimp, thawed if frozen
2 hard-boiled eggs roughly chopped
2 tablespoons finely chopped fresh parsley
salt and freshly ground black pepper
thick lemon wedges, to garnish (optional)

1 Put the smoked fish in a large saucepan, cover with cold water and bring to a boil. Lower the heat, cover the pan, and simmer gently 10 minutes, until the fish flakes easily when pierced with a sharp knife.

2 Remove the fish with a slotted spoon, reserving the poaching liquid in the pan. Leave the fish until cool enough to handle, then flake the flesh into small pieces, discarding the skin and any remaining bones.

3 Make the fish poaching liquid up to 4½ cups with water. Bring to a boil, add the rice, cover and simmer 15 to 40 minutes until tender. Turn into a strainer and leave to drain.

4 Meanwhile, melt the butter in a separate large saucepan, add the onion and cook gently 5 minutes until soft and lightly colored. Stir in the mixed vegetables and cover the pan. Continue cooking over low heat 5 minutes, shaking the pan from time to time.

5 Add the flaked fish and drained rice to the vegetables, with the yogurt, lemon juice, mussels, shrimp, hard-boiled eggs and parsley. Season to taste with salt and pepper. Taking care not to break up the ingredients, fork through lightly over gentle heat until well mixed and heated through.

6 Pile the kedgeree into a warmed serving dish, garnish the ends of the dish with lemon wedges, if liked and serve at once.

Cook's Notes

TIME
Preparation of fish and cooking take about 1 hour.

DID YOU KNOW
Smoking is actually one of the oldest methods of preserving food. Nowadays, however, the process is used more for the unique flavor it imparts.

There are 2 ways of smoking fish: Hot-smoking and cold-smoking. The first produces cooked fish that is ready to eat. Salmon, trout and mackerel can be hot-smoked. Cold-smoking is done at a much lower temperature and the fish needs to be cooked before eating (e.g. cod, haddock and kippers).

• 500 calories per portion

Seafood and orange kabobs

SERVES 4
1 lb tilefish fillet, skinned and cut into 1-inch cubes
½ lb unshelled shrimp
4 large oranges
watercress sprigs, to garnish

MARINADE
¼ cup vegetable oil
¼ cup lemon juice
½ teaspoon dried marjoram
1 large clove garlic, crushed (optional)
salt and freshly ground black pepper

1 Combine all the marinade ingredients in a large shallow dish. Add the tilefish cubes and shrimp and turn to coat (see Cook's tip). Leave to marinate 30 minutes at room temperature.
2 Meanwhile, peel and segment the oranges over the marinade, so that any juice drips into it. Set the orange segments aside on a plate.
3 Line the broiler pan with a piece of foil. Preheat the broiler to moderate.
4 Remove the tilefish cubes and shrimp from the marinade and thread them and the orange segments onto 4 oiled long kabob skewers (see Preparation).
5 Place the kabobs on the broiler pan and brush well with some of the marinade. Broil about 5 minutes, then turn the kabobs and broil a further 5 minutes, brushing once or twice with more marinade. [!]
6 Arrange the cooked kabobs on a warmed large serving plate. Brush with marinade, garnish with watercress sprigs and serve at once.

Cook's Notes

TIME
Preparation takes 20-25 minutes. Allow 30 minutes for marinating. Cooking the kabobs takes about 10 minutes.

PREPARATION
When threading the shrimp onto the kabob skewers, push the skewer through the thickest part of the body so that they do not fall off during cooking.

COOK'S TIP
If you prefer not to shell the cooked shrimp at the table, broil shelled jumbo shrimp on the kabobs instead.

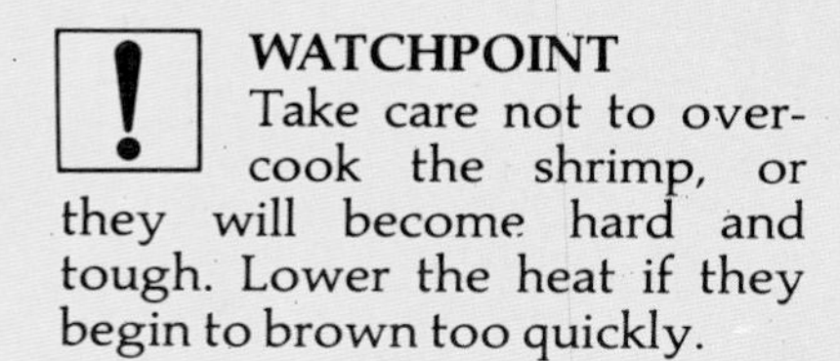

WATCHPOINT
Take care not to overcook the shrimp, or they will become hard and tough. Lower the heat if they begin to brown too quickly.

● 270 calories per portion

Kidney and orange simmer

SERVES 4

1 lb lamb kidneys, skinned and chopped, with cores removed (see Buying guide)
1 tablespoon vegetable oil
1 onion, chopped
1 clove garlic, crushed (optional)
1¼ cups chicken broth
1 tablespoon white wine vinegar
pinch of dry mustard
pinch of cayenne
2 teaspoons chopped fresh tarragon
finely grated rind of 1 orange
1 tablespoon orange juice
¼ lb mushrooms, sliced
salt and freshly ground black pepper

TO GARNISH
1 tablespoon chopped fresh parsley
orange slices

1 Heat the oil in a large skillet with a top, add the onion and garlic, if using, and cook over moderate heat 1-2 minutes. Add the kidneys to the pan and cook a further 2-3 minutes, stirring all the time.

2 Stir the broth, vinegar, mustard, cayenne and tarragon into the pan, with the grated orange rind and juice. Add the mushrooms, stir well and season to taste with salt and pepper.

3 Bring to a boil, then lower the heat, cover the pan and simmer for 15 minutes until the kidneys are tender.

4 Transfer to a warmed serving dish, sprinkle with parsley and garnish with orange slices. Serve at once, piping hot.

TIME
Preparation takes 10 minutes, cooking about 20 minutes.

BUYING GUIDE
Kidneys go "off" very quickly and must be eaten the day they are bought. Frozen kidneys may be used but must be thawed completely before using.

SPECIAL OCCASION
Stir in 2 tablespoons light cream just before serving.

SERVING IDEAS
Serve with plain boiled white rice. This is a rich dish, which is best served with a simple green salad.

● 150 calories per portion

Kidney and pork medley

SERVES 4

4 lamb kidneys, halved and cores removed
½ lb lean pork fillet, cut into 1-inch cubes
2 tablespoons vegetable oil
1 onion, chopped
1 can (about 12 oz) tomatoes, peeled and quartered
3 tablespoons sweet red vermouth
½ teaspoon dried oregano
salt and freshly ground black pepper
⅔ cup plain yogurt

1 Heat the oil in a large saucepan, then add the onion and cook very gently 5 minutes until soft and lightly colored.

2 Add the pork to the pan and cook turning from time to time, 10 minutes until lightly browned.

3 Cut each kidney half into 4 pieces. Add to the pan and cook, stirring frequently, 5 minutes,

4 Stir in the tomatoes, vermouth and oregano, and season to taste with salt and pepper. Cover and cook 10 minutes, then remove the top and cook a further 5 minutes until the pork is tender when pierced with a sharp knife.

5 Remove from the heat, taste and adjust seasoning, then swirl in the yogurt. Turn into a warmed serving dish and serve at once.

Cook's Notes

TIME
Preparation and cooking take 40 minutes.

SERVING IDEAS
Serve with boiled noodles or rice and a fresh green vegetable such as broccoli. Or, use as a topping for jacket-baked potatoes (it will serve 8 this way). Alternatively, try using as a tasty stuffing for a baked squash.

ECONOMY
Chicken broth may be used as a substitute for the red vermouth.

VARIATIONS
Add ¼ lb button mushrooms, quartered and cooked in butter, just before serving. Substitute dried sage for the oregano.

● 250 calories per portion

Liver loaf

SERVES 6
1 lb lamb liver, trimmed and sliced
1 tablespoon vegetable oil
½ lb pork sausagemeat
⅔ cup fresh white bread crumbs
1 large onion, grated
1 tablespoon Worcestershire sauce
2 small eggs, beaten
1 teaspoon dried thyme
salt and freshly ground black pepper

TOMATO SAUCE
1 tablespoon vegetable oil
1 small onion, finely chopped
1 clove garlic, crushed (optional)
1 can (about 14 oz) tomatoes
⅔ cup water
1 teaspoon tomato paste
½ teaspoon sugar
½ teaspoon dried sweet basil

TO GARNISH
1-2 tomatoes, sliced
parsley sprigs

1 Preheat the oven to 350°.
2 Grease an 8½ × 4½ × 2½ inch loaf pan. Heat the oil in a skillet, add the liver and cook over brisk heat until browned on all sides. Remove with a slotted spoon. Drain and cool on paper towels, then grind.
3 Mix in the ground liver with all the remaining ingredients, adding salt and pepper to taste. Make sure that all the ingredients are combined.
4 Spoon the mixture into the prepared pan pressing it down firmly. Cover with foil, then place the loaf pan in a roasting pan half filled with hot water.
5 Bake in the oven about 1 hour or until the juices run clear when the loaf is pierced in the center with a knife.
6 Meanwhile, make the tomato sauce: Heat the oil in a saucepan, add the onion and garlic (if using) and cook gently until soft. Add the remaining sauce ingredients with salt and pepper to taste, then bring to a boil, stirring constantly to break up the tomatoes.
7 Lower the heat, half cover with a top and simmer gently about 20 minutes, stirring from time to time. Remove from the heat, leave to cool for a few minutes, then purée in a blender or work through a strainer. Return to the pan, taste and adjust seasoning, then simmer gently on top of the stove until cooked.
8 Remove the cooked liver loaf from the roasting pan, leave to stand 5 minutes, [!] then pour off any fat and juices from the pan.
9 Turn the loaf out onto a warmed serving platter then pour a little of the hot tomato sauce over the top (see Variation). Serve at once, with the remaining sauce passed separately in a gravyboat.

Cook's Notes

TIME
25 minutes preparation, plus about 1 hour baking. Allow an extra 5-10 minutes for turning out.

FREEZING
Leave until cold, then unmold, wrap in plastic wrap and overwrap in a freezer bag. Seal, label and freeze up to 3 months. Thaw in wrappings overnight in the refrigerator.

● 385 calories per portion

VARIATION
Use about ¼ cup instant mashed potato mix made according to package directions, to cover the loaf. Pipe it over, or use a fork to mark it decoratively. Garnish with tomatoes and parsley.

WATCHPOINT
The loaf must be left to stand in the pan for at least 5 minutes after cooking to allow the mixture to settle. If the loaf is turned out immediately it will be difficult to slice neatly.

Liver and bacon hotpot

SERVES 4

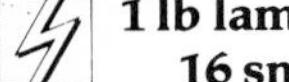

1 lb lamb, calves or pig liver, cut into 16 small slices
1 tablespoon vegetable oil
2 tablespoons butter or margarine
2 medium onions, sliced into thin rings
4 bacon slices
1 green apple, pared, cored and sliced
salt and freshly ground black pepper
few drops Worcestershire sauce
1¼ cups hot beef broth
1 teaspoon cornstarch

1 Preheat the oven to 350°.
2 Heat oil and butter in a large skillet and cook the liver slices over moderate heat until brown on both sides. Remove with a slotted spoon and transfer to a plate.
3 Lower the heat and cook the onion rings 5 to 10 minutes. Spread the onion evenly over the base of an ovenproof serving dish.
4 Sandwich ½ slice of bacon between 2 apple slices and 2 liver slices. Turn the liver sandwiches on their sides and arrange in rows on top of the onions. Sprinkle with salt and pepper.
5 Add a few drops of Worcestershire sauce to the broth. Blend the cornstarch to a paste in a small saucepan with a little cold water, then gradually stir in the broth. Bring to a boil stirring constantly, then lower the heat and simmer gently until thickened. Pour over the liver.
6 Cover and bake in the oven about 30 minutes. [!] Serve hot, straight from the serving dish.

Cook's Notes

TIME
An easy dish taking less than an hour.

COOK'S TIP
If using pig liver, soak it in a little milk for about an hour to remove the strong flavor. Drain and dry it before cooking.

WATCHPOINT
Always use liver on the day it is bought, or within 24 hours if kept well wrapped in a refrigerator. Do not be tempted to leave the liver in the oven for longer than 30 minutes – overcooked liver is tough and leathery, and the apple slices will disintegrate.

SERVING IDEAS
Serve with creamy mashed potatoes – made extra special with a large knob of butter, a few tablespoons of cream and a beaten egg. Beat them well until soft and fluffy.

● 365 calories per portion

Liver cobbler

SERVES 4
¾ lb lamb liver, cut into bite-sized pieces
1¼ cups milk
1 tablespoon all-purpose flour
salt and freshly ground black pepper
¼ cup butter or margarine
6 streaky bacon slices, cut into thin strips
2 large onions, sliced
1 can (about 8 oz) tomatoes
½ teaspoon dried mixed herbs

TOPPING
2 cups self-rising flour
pinch of salt
¼ cup butter or margarine, diced
½ teaspoon dried mixed herbs
⅔ cup milk
a little milk, to glaze

1 Put the liver pieces in a shallow dish, pour over the milk and leave to marinate at room temperature 1 hour (see Cook's tip).
2 Remove the liver from the milk and dry on paper towels. Spread out the flour on a flat plate and season with salt and pepper. Dip the liver strips in the seasoned flour, turning them to coat thoroughly.
3 Melt the butter in a skillet add the bacon and onions and cook gently 5 minutes until soft. Remove with a slotted spoon and put in a round 9 inch diameter deep casserole dish.
4 Add the liver to the skillet and cook 1-2 minutes, turning the pieces to seal.
5 Gradually stir the milk into the pan and bring to a boil, stirring. Cook 2-3 minutes.
6 Using a slotted spoon, transfer the liver to the casserole with the onions and bacon. Pour in the milk and stir in the tomatoes with their juice and herbs. Season to taste with salt and pepper.
7 Preheat the oven to 425°.
8 Make the cobbler topping: Sift the flour and salt into a bowl. Add the butter and cut it into the flour with the fingertips until the mixture resembles fine bread crumbs. Add the herbs and gradually mix in the milk to form a soft dough.

9 Turn the dough onto a lightly floured surface and knead gently until smooth. Roll out to about ½-inch thickness. Cut into rounds, using a 2½-inch cutter.
10 Arrange the rounds of dough overlapping in a circle on top of the liver mixture in the casserole. Brush the dough topping with a little milk to glaze.
11 Bake the cobbler in the oven 20-25 minutes until the topping is well risen and golden brown. Serve at once, straight from the casserole.

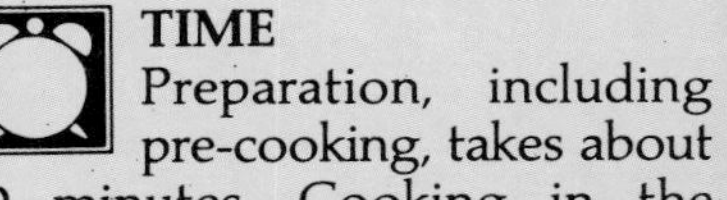

TIME
Preparation, including pre-cooking, takes about 30 minutes. Cooking in the oven takes 20-25 minutes, but allow 1 hour for the liver to marinate in the milk.

COOK'S TIP
Marinating the liver in milk makes it beautifully tender, and the milk also gives a deliciously creamy sauce.

VARIATION
Add 1 can (about 7½ oz) mushrooms drained, to the liver mixture.

SERVING IDEAS
Serve the cobbler with carrots and green beans. The topping is starchy, so there is no need for a potato accompaniment.

• 770 calories per portion

Chinese-style liver

SERVES 4-5

1½ lb lamb or calves liver, trimmed and thinly sliced (see Preparation)
4 tablespoons vegetable oil
12 large scallions, cut into ½-inch lengths (see Preparation)
¼ lb mushrooms, sliced
2 tablespoons dry or medium sherry
1-2 tablespoons soy sauce
1 tablespoon wine vinegar
1 teaspoon sugar
½ teaspoon ground ginger
2 tablespoons cornstarch
2 cups water
thin carrot strips, to garnish

MARINADE
1 teaspoon salt
½ teaspoon freshly ground black pepper
4 teaspoons cornstarch
4 teaspoons dry sherry
4 teaspoons vegetable oil

1 To make the marinade: Mix the marinade ingredients together in a large bowl. Add the sliced liver, stir well and leave 10 minutes.
2 Heat 3 tablespoons oil in a large saucepan over moderate heat. Drain the liver and add to the pan. Stir-fry (see Did you know) over high heat 2-3 minutes only, until the liver is browned all over. Remove from the pan with a slotted spoon, and reserve.
3 Heat the remaining tablespoon oil in the pan, add the scallions and mushrooms and stir-fry over high heat 1 minute.
4 Remove the pan from the heat and stir in the sherry, soy sauce, wine vinegar, sugar and ginger.
5 In a large bowl, mix the cornstarch to a paste with a little of the water. Gradually stir in remaining water.
6 Return the pan to the heat and bring to a boil, scraping up all the sediment from the sides and bottom of the pan with a wooden spoon.
7 Stir in the cornstarch mixture, add the liver and bring to a boil, stirring. Simmer gently 2 minutes. Transfer the mixture to a warmed serving dish (see Serving ideas). Garnish with carrot strips and serve at once.

Cook's Notes

TIME
Preparation and cooking takes 30 minutes.

PREPARATION
Slice the liver no more than ¼-inch thick, or it will not cook in the specified time.

To trim the scallions: Remove the outside layer of each one, cut off most of the green part and slice off the root.

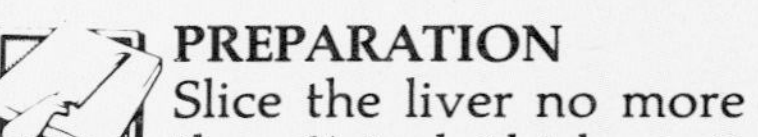

DID YOU KNOW
Stir-frying is a term frequently used in Chinese cooking. It means literally stirring and frying at the same time. The ingredients are kept on the move over high heat so that they cook quickly and evenly.

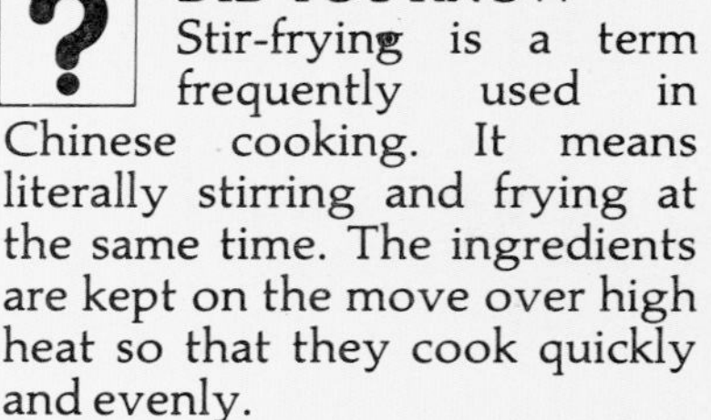

SERVING IDEAS
Serve with boiled rice or noodles, and a stir-fried vegetable accompaniment.

● 495 calories per portion

INDEX

Picture credits
Theo Bergstrom: 24
Martin Brigdale: 21, 54, 68
Paul Bussell: 23, 79
Alan Duns: 27, 36, 65, 72, 75
John Elliot: 14, 48
Edmund Goldspink: 30
James Jackson: 11, 19, 28, 34, 39, 51, 52, 55, 61, 77
Michael Kay: 37, 40
Paul Kemp: 80
Chris Knaggs: 25, 35, 38, 41
Bob Komar: 53, 69
Don Last: 18, 29, 74, 81
Fred Mancini: 4, 7, 31, 58
Peter Mayers: 5, 13, 16, 20, 26, 43, 44, 50, 59, 66
Roger Phillips: 15, 63, 73, 76
Roger Tuft: 32, 60
Paul Webster: 6, 9, 12, 17, 33, 45, 47, 56, 57, 64, 70, 78
Paul Williams: 8, 22, 49, 67, 71
John Woodcock: 10
Graham Young: 46